Walking on & around the Staffordshire Way

Edited by Geoff Loadwick

SIGMA Leisure

Published by Sigma Leisure – an imprint of
Sigma Press, 1 South Oak Lane, Wilmslow, Cheshire SK9 6AR, England.

British Library Cataloguing in Publication Data
A CIP record for this book is available from the British Library.

ISBN: 1-85058-594-6

Typesetting and Design by: Sigma Press, Wilmslow, Cheshire.

Cover photograph: A family ramble along the towpath at Denford

Maps: Rob Cox

Photographs: Geoff Loadwick

Printed by: MFP Design and Print

Acknowledgements

This book owes its existence to those dedicated ramblers who have given their own precious leisure time so that others may enjoy these walks. Without their enthusiasm and their careful checking and re-checking of the routes, this book could not have been produced. In addition to the contributors who are acknowledged in the walk description headings, I would like to thank John Allen for suggesting the route of the Kinver walk, and Jack Price for his comments relating to the old roads near Wolverhampton mentioned in the Perton walk. I am grateful for the invaluable help given by Rob and Celia Cox, Bob Foulkes, Fred Price, Harry Scott, Vera and David Wilkinson, John Youens, and above all by my wife, Margaret, who have painstakingly assisted in checking the walk descriptions. I am also grateful to Rob Cox for drawing the maps.

Canal towpaths, which form important links in several of the walks, are the property of British Waterways. I am indebted to Ian Selby, Waterway Manager for the British Waterways' Pennine and Potteries Waterway, and to Roger Herrington, Waterway Manager for the British Waterways' Shropshire Union, Staffordshire & Worcestershire and Trent & Mersey Canals, who have granted us permission to include stretches of towpaths in some of our route descriptions.

All profits earned from this book will be used by Staffordshire Area of the Ramblers' Association to improve the footpath network for the benefit of the rambling community.

Contents

Useful Information

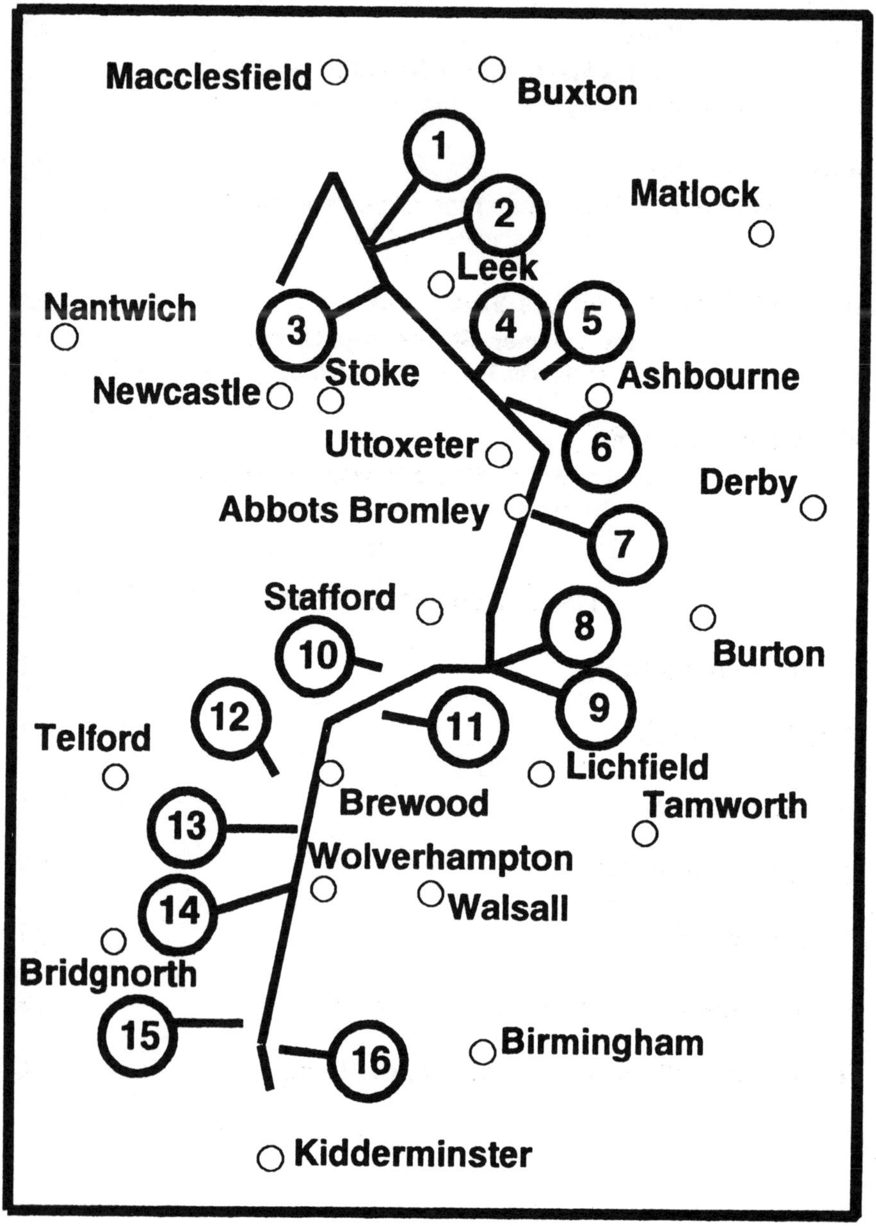

Location Map for the Walks

Introduction

The Staffordshire Way

The Staffordshire Way covers a distance of 92 miles, spanning Staffordshire between the rugged gritstone hills in the north and the gentler landscaped parklands of the south. It passes through some of the county's most attractive scenery and most interesting towns and villages. It was created and developed by Staffordshire County Council between 1977 and 1983, and in 1978 was commended by the British Tourist Authority for being one of the best new tourist facilities of the year. Although the Way is not designated by the Countryside Commission as a national long distance path, it is recognised to be of major recreational importance.

The Way traces a route through the fascinating social, religious, and industrial history of the county. It passes ancient hill forts, Roman settlements, and more recent wartime airfields and encampments. It makes use of medieval sunken lanes and old coach roads and follows canal towpaths and the track-beds of former railway lines. It passes the sites of early corn mills, a flint mill, a smelting mill and a wireworks. It visits primitive houses that have been cut out of solid rock and passes through the grounds of stately mansions.

Another of the Way's attractions is the stunning diversity of landscape which is steadily revealed to the walker. Starting from the gritstone ridge on the edge of the Peak District in the north, passing between the wooded hills of Cannock Chase, an area of Outstanding Natural Beauty, and continuing via landscaped parklands in the south to end, on a high, at Kinver Edge.

Circular walks

Many ramblers who aspire to walk the Staffordshire Way from end to end, dream of devoting a week or so of their annual holidays to it. In reality, family commitments and a lack of time or of physical fitness, often conspire to ensure that the dream remains just a dream. Alternative strategies for walking the Way, depend on completing the walk in stages, and arranging private transport at the start and finish of each stage. Such strategies often include time constraints and put unacceptable limits on a walker's freedom to choose the right pace for the occasion. Circular walks offer what many consider to be a preferable solution, and the walks in this book cover a varied selection of some of the best sections of the Way.

The Ramblers' Association

The contributors are all experienced members of the Ramblers' Association. The Association was formed in 1935, and now has over 117,000 members, of whom more than 2,600 belong to the Staffordshire Area covering Staffordshire, Stoke-on-Trent, and the Metropolitan Boroughs of Dudley, Sandwell, Walsall, and Wolverhampton. The Association seeks to help everyone to enjoy walking in the countryside, to foster care and understanding of the countryside, to protect rights of way, to secure public access on foot to open country, and to defend the natural beauty of the countryside.

The origin of this book

1995 marked the 60th anniversary of the Association and in casting around for a suitable project to mark the jubilee, the Staffordshire Area of the Association resolved to undertake a very ambitious task; to refurbish the whole of the Staffordshire Way. Attention had became focused on the Staffordshire Way because the official guidebook and accommodation list were becoming out of date and more and more walkers were reporting problems with worn out stiles and bridges, and with poor waymarking. At that time, Staffordshire Area of the Ramblers comprised eight groups. Each group agreed to survey up to twelve miles of the Way and to set up working parties. They had the support of the

County Council which, whilst openly admitting that it lacked sufficient resources to put the Way in order by itself, readily agreed to supply materials, tools and a set of detailed maps. Other local organisations also lent their support and the Ramblers were helped by parish councils, Girl Guides, the British Trust for Conservation Volunteers, Staffordshire Wildlife Trust, British Waterways and numerous other landowners and farmers.

Teams of volunteers cleared a total of ten miles of overgrown paths, and repaired or installed 24 stiles and gates. They refurbished five bridges, erected or reinstated 23 signposts, and nailed hundreds of waymarks to posts. An accommodation guide with 80 addresses within two miles of the Way was produced and over seventy suggestions to update the guidebook were presented to the County Council. By Sunday, 24 September 1995, everything was in place for a celebratory walk along the Way; each group covering its own stretch of path.

This book has its origins in the jubilee project. Many of the contributors took part in the project and are keen to encourage others to discover the delights of walking the Staffordshire Way.

Maps

All the walk descriptions have been carefully written and assume that users are not necessarily skilled in map reading or compass work. Those users who are competent at map reading know how much more enjoyment and satisfaction can be gained before, during, and after a walk by studying its route on the map. They also know that they are better prepared if, for any reason, they need to abandon a walk. Details of appropriate maps are given at the head of each walk description. The sketch maps that accompany each walk merely give an indication of the route, they are not drawn to any particular scale, and they are no substitute for an Ordnance Survey map. The numbers on the sketch maps correspond to paragraph numbers in the text and will help users to relate the written description to the map.

Grid references

The starting point of each walk is described in words and by a six-figure grid reference at the head of each walk description. The marginal information at the edge of Ordnance Survey maps describes how to take a grid reference. All Ordnance Survey maps are criss-crossed by vertical and horizontal grid lines which, if they were drawn on the ground would be exactly one kilometre apart. On the map, grid lines are 4 centimetres apart on the 1:25 000 scale and 2 centimetres apart on the 1:50 000 scale. At the end of each grid line there is a two-digit number written at the margin of the map. The vertical lines which define the *eastings* in a grid reference are numbered at the top and bottom margins. The horizontal lines, which provide the *northings*, are numbered on the left and right margins. A four-figure grid reference defines a particular kilometre square.

For example the grid square defined by the four-digit number 0420, is the square with a grid line on the left (its easting) numbered 04 and a grid line along the bottom (its northing) numbered 20. Thus a four-figure grid reference defines a square with a side of 1000 metres (= 1 kilometre).

To decode a six-figure grid reference, first split the number into two groups of three. e.g. 046203 becomes 046 203. The first two numbers of each group define a 1 kilometre square on the Ordnance Survey map by locating its left boundary and lower boundary, as described above. In this case the square 0420. The two remaining single digits define a square with a side of 100 metres within the one kilometre

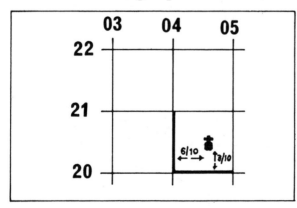

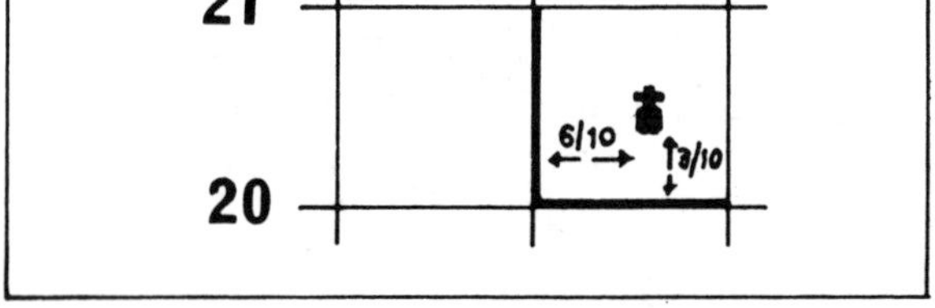

A six-figure grid reference

square. The final digit in the left group defines the number of tenths (100 metres) from the left edge, the last digit in the right group, the number of tenths from the bottom edge. Thus in the figure, the church with a tower has a six-figure grid reference of 046203.

When quoting a grid reference, for confirmation and to guard against error, it is good practice to say what the reference refers to: e.g. "the church at grid reference 046203". A full reference would additionally have two prefix letters e.g. SK046203 but these are not necessary when the appropriate Ordnance Survey map is being used.

The paths used in these walks

Many of the routes follow waymarked paths, but not all paths are waymarked and waymarks can be misleading. They should only be used with caution. The Staffordshire Way sometimes follows concessionary footpaths, that is it sometimes uses paths which although not statutory rights of way can nevertheless be walked because the landowner has given permission. Apart from the concessionary paths used on the Staffordshire Way, and some lengths of canal towpath, all the paths except one, in the walk descriptions are believed to be definitive rights of way. The exception is a short stretch of well-used footpath across waste ground behind houses, at the end of the Perton walk. Its use avoids several hundred metres of verge-side walking along a busy road.

Problems encountered on public paths

Despite the provisions of the Rights of Way Act 1990, the laws on ploughing public paths are still ignored by some farmers. If a path runs around the edge of a field it must not be ploughed or disturbed. If a path runs across a field, the farmer is allowed to plough or disturb the surface when cultivating the land for a crop. But the farmer is obliged to carry out restoration works, normally within 24 hours of the disturbance, unless it is the first disturbance for a crop, when 14 days are allowed. After restoration, the surface should be reasonably convenient to use and the line of the path should be apparent on the ground. Crops, except grass, must not be allowed to grow on, or extend over the path.

If you meet a problem when following a public footpath, please report it to the local authority's countryside officer. An example of a form, suitable for making such a report to Staffordshire County Council is given in the ***Useful Information*** section at the end of this book. The authority will need to know the date the problem was encountered, what the problem was and exactly where it was. The authority has a duty to enforce the law. It can give notice to the farmer to put matters right, and if necessary it can do the work itself and send the farmer the bill. The legal line of the path stays the same even if it is obscured or obstructed by ploughing or crops. It is better to keep to the correct line wherever possible, but if the path is blocked, find a convenient way round, taking care to shut any gates and to avoid damaging walls or fences.

The Country code

For years, walkers in the countryside have been asked to obey the country code. Ramblers' adherence to it makes for a more cordial relationship with farmers and landowners without whose cooperation, walking in the countryside would be a far less pleasurable pastime.

- Enjoy the countryside and respect its life and work.
- Guard against all risk of fire.
- Fasten all gates.
- Keep your dogs under close control.
- Keep to public paths across farmland.
- Use gates and stiles to cross fences, hedges and walls.
- Leave livestock, crops and machinery alone.
- Take your litter home.

- ¤ Help to keep all water clean.
- ¤ Protect wildlife, plants and trees.
- ¤ Take special care on country roads.
- ¤ Make no unnecessary noise.

It seems only fair that there should be an equivalent code for farmers and landowners. Here is one version:

- ¤ Welcome visitors to the countryside and respect their use of public paths.
- ¤ Ensure that gates and stiles on public paths are safe and easy to use.
- ¤ Insulate electric fences where they cross public paths.
- ¤ Keep dogs under control and protect path users from dangerous animals.
- ¤ Respect signposts and waymarks.
- ¤ Comply with the Rights of Way Act 1990:
- ¤ Do not leave litter.
- ¤ Help to keep all water clean.
- ¤ Protect wildlife, plants and trees.
- ¤ Take special care on country roads.
- ¤ Make no unnecessary noise.

Walk 1: The Cloud

Tony Adair, Stoke/Newcastle Group

Starting point: Grid Reference SJ 936623, Rushton Spencer Staffordshire Way picnic area car park, next to the former railway station. Travelling from Leek along the A523 towards Macclesfield, turn left just before Caverswall Motors filling station and turn left again just after the Knott Inn. Other possible starting points, on or close to the circuit, are Biddulph Grange country park and Timbersbrook picnic site.

Distance: 12 miles (19 kilometres)

Useful maps: Ordnance Survey Pathfinder 792 Kidsgrove and Leek, and Pathfinder 776 Congleton, or Ordnance Survey Landranger 118 Stoke-on-Trent and Macclesfield.

Terrain: Moderate hills and flat stretches, fine views in numerous places around all points of the compass.

---

1. From the car park turn right onto the former railway line to follow it south. Go under the first bridge and turn immediately left up the path on the embankment to a stile, cross the stile and turn left to go over the bridge. Head up the hill to the church and some trees.

The church is St Lawrence's at Rushton which dates from 1203. The small church door to the south has a date of 1713 and inside can be detected the remains of an earlier timber-framed structure. Amongst the graves in the churchyard will be found that of Wilfred Gibson, the last Rushton station-master.

Go through an iron gate into the churchyard. Follow the path around the church to the main gate and exit onto a tarmac roadway. Follow the road away from the church to a finger post, turn left and head downhill to the far right hand corner

St Lawrence's church, Rushton

of the field where there is a stile and a stream. Cross the stream and follow the hedge on your right to a stone squeezer stile just to the left of the field corner. Go over the stile and cross the field to the next stile in the hedge opposite. Go over this stile and follow the fence line on your right to a stile giving access to the road at the side of the Crown Inn car park.

2. Cross the road to a stile in the hedge opposite, slightly to the right. Go over the stile and walk through three fields towards a house and an iron gate. Go through the gate and turn right down a track to a road. Turn left at the road and go downhill and over a bridge. Immediately after the bridge there are two gates on the left; go through the second gate and head up the middle of the field to pass under power cables, and continue straight on to a stile in a low wall ahead. Go through the stile and turn slightly left towards a single oak and a stile in the hedge. Cross over the stile and head diagonally right to follow a hedge line to the far right corner of the field and pass over a stile next to a gate. Walk towards the right hand side of the

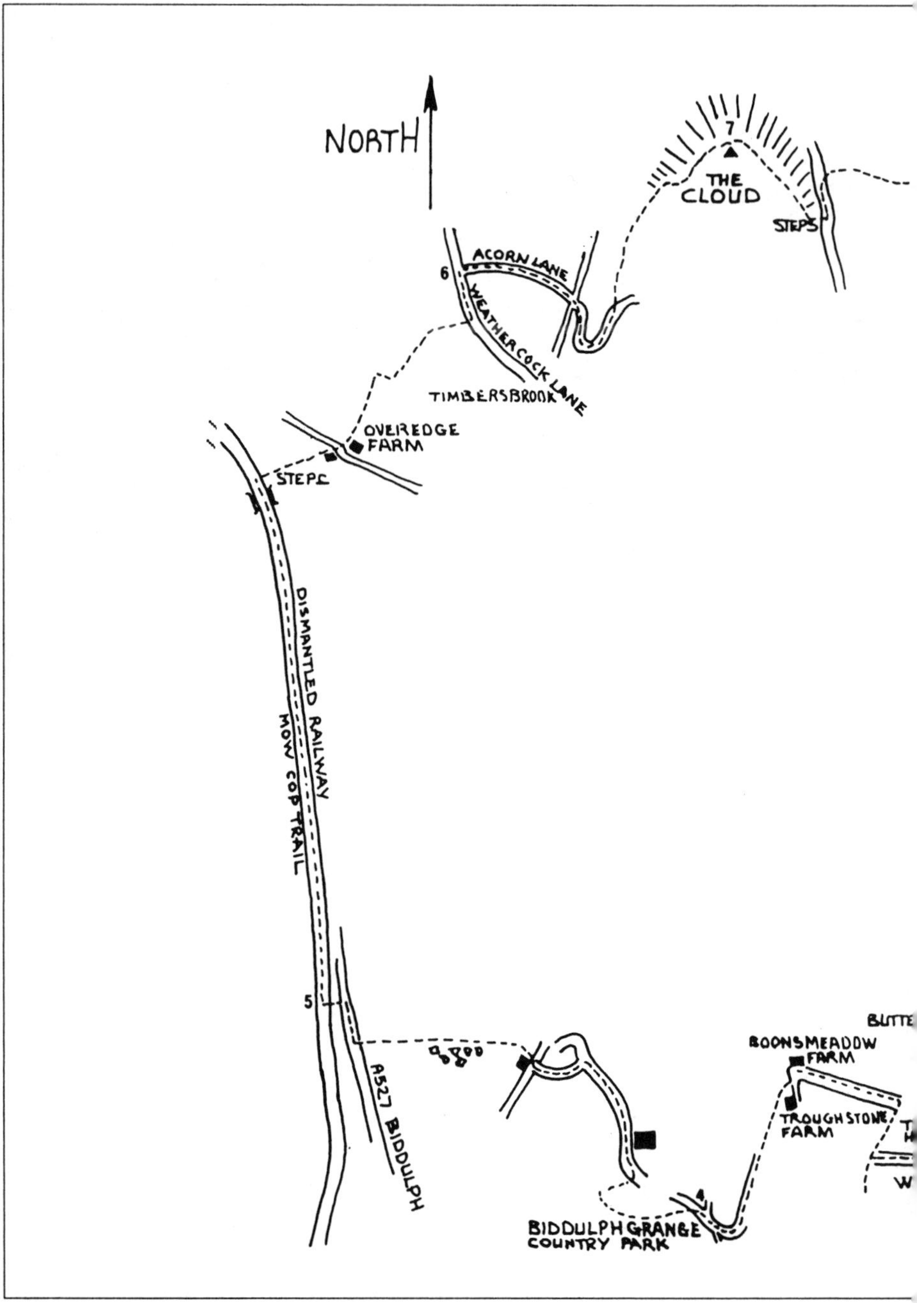
NORTH
7
THE CLOUD
STEPS
6
ACORN LANE
WEATHERCOCK LANE
TIMBERSBROOK
OVEREDGE FARM
STEPS
DISMANTLED RAILWAY
MOW COP TRAIL
5
A527 BIDDULPH
BOONSMEADOW FARM
TROUGHSTONE FARM
4
BIDDULPH GRANGE COUNTRY PARK

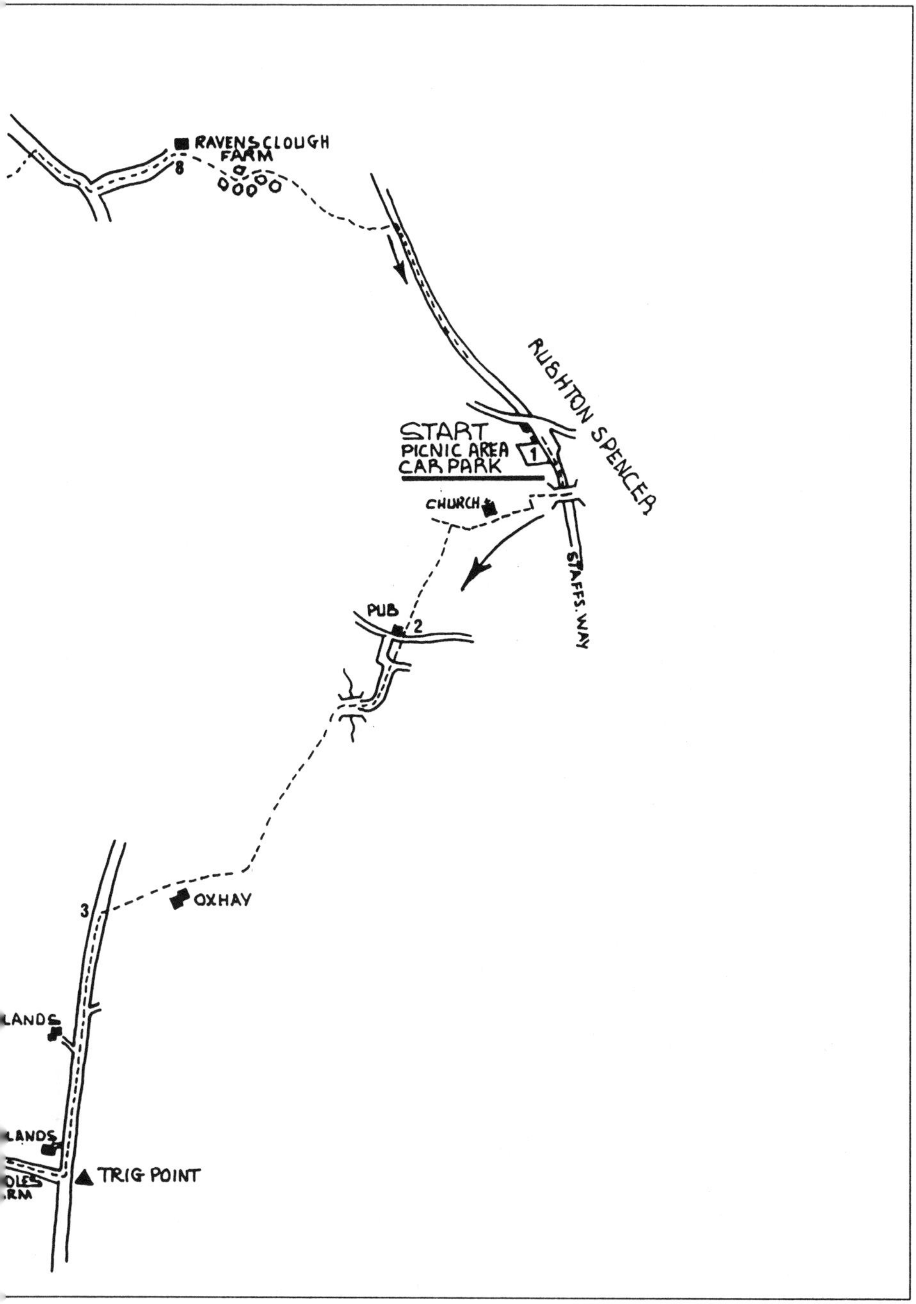
RAVENSCLOUGH FARM
8
RUSHTON SPENCER
START
PICNIC AREA
CAR PARK
1
CHURCH
STAFFS. WAY
PUB
2
3
OXHAY
LANDS
LANDS
TRIG POINT

farm buildings ahead but before reaching the buildings, cross the stile on the corner at the left hand end of a low stone wall. Follow the hedge line up the hill, cross a farm road and continue up the hill through a stone squeezer stile. Continue up the hill following the boundary on the left through three fields. At the end of the wall on the left, continue straight up the field to the road and turn left.

The views to the north and north-east take in Bosley Reservoir, Croker Hill with its tower, and Shutlingsloe. The Roaches can be seen to the east-north-east.

3. Continue along the road following the gently rising ridge, and ignoring roads to the left and right. At the top of the hill there is a triangulation pillar in a field on the left. Turn right at the pillar into a lane, called "The Hollands". Pass Wardle's Farm on the left and at the end of the lane turn right onto a track which is a public footpath. Continue along the track, passing to the right of a low building, to reach a gate. Go through the gate and continue along the track following it round a left hand bend to a gate and stile giving access to a tarmac lane. Where the lane turns sharply to the right, opposite a farm, turn left along a lane towards Troughstone Farm. At the first gate, go over a stile on the right and cross the field diagonally left to the corner of a wall that juts out. Follow the wall round to the next corner, cross the stile and soon after, cross another stile. Follow the path skirting around the hill to a gap stile next to a gate. Go through the stile and continue around the hill to a stile in the wall. Turn left and walk down the ridge, keeping a wall on the left, to a track. Walk down the track to a road, and continue downhill to reach some posts protecting a grassy verge on the left. Just beyond the posts, go through the stile on the left into Biddulph Grange Country Park.

4. Go down the steps, at the bottom turn right and follow the stream down, crossing and re-crossing the stream in the descent. At the stone bridge with low walls, turn right to cross over the stream and walk up a path to a junction. Take the path up the steps to Hurst Road. Turn left down Hurst Road, passing to the left of the quarry buildings. Continue down the road and after passing to the left of a large, grey, stone house called *Hollyhurst*, turn down the first lane on the left, just before Hurst Road turns sharply to the left. At the end of the lane, cross a stile on the right and soon afterwards cross a stile and a stream into a football field and follow the hedgeline on the right boundary into the *Talbot* Inn car park. Cross the car park, go over the road to a telephone box and go down some steps in the wall to the right of the box. Pass to the left of the pond and follow the track round to the left. Pass over a small bridge and go through a stile into a field.

There is a good view of Congleton Edge ahead

Keep to the right of the wood and follow the path downhill, through two stiles, under some power cables, and through a gate at the bottom of the field onto the A527, Biddulph – Congleton road. Turn right and follow the road to a lane on the left, signposted to Congleton Edge. Cross the main road with care and go along the lane to a stile on the right just before a bridge. Go over the stile and up the steps onto the Staffordshire Way.

5. Turn right and walk along the former railway. After 1 mile (1.5 kilometres), the track-bed crosses an iron bridge over Reade's Lane by a cottage on the right.

Before Reade's Lane is crossed, the track-bed crosses the A527 road. By leaving the route temporarily at this point, refreshment can be obtained at the *Castle* Inn.

Just over a quarter of a mile (0.5 kilometre) beyond Reade's Lane the track crosses a concrete bridge over a narrow underpass. Fifty metres afterwards, go down some wooden steps on the right to a stile and a footpath sign. Cross over the stile, turn left and follow the railway fence to the field corner. Turn right before a stile and follow the hedge on your left passing through a farmyard onto Brookhouse Lane. Turn right and walk along the road for 50 metres and leave it from the left at a footpath sign. Cross a small paddock and go through a squeezer stile; then, with the farm on your right, cross two fields. At the next field cross a dip in the ground and veer slightly to the right to reach a stile in the far field boundary. Go over the stile and cross the next field to a stile above Timbersbrook. Cross the footbridge and go along the side of an old mill into a rough road leading to Weather Cock Lane.

6. Turn left and walk along the lane. After 250 metres, turn right up a green lane, Acorn Lane. At the top of the lane cross the road into Gosberryhole Lane and follow it to the National Trust sign where the lane forks. Take the left fork up the stony track and follow it uphill to a stone wall in front of a plantation. Bear left and follow the path along the escarpment to the triangulation pillar at the Cloud summit.

From here there are good views in fine weather. In the sweep to the north, north-west and west can be seen the Cheshire plain with Jodrell Bank radio telescope and Ellesmere Port power station. Rudyard reservoir can be seen to the south-east and Mow Cop, the start of the Staffordshire Way, can be seen to the south-west.

7. Continue past the triangulation pillar with the escarpment on the left and go down the hill for a quarter of a mile (0.5 kilometre) and descend the steps to a rough road. Turn left and walk down the road to emerge at a road at Cloud Side. Turn left and walk down the road for 200 metres to a small clump of trees on a roadside bank on the right. Climb the bank and go over a stile. Follow the field boundary on the right through two fields. At the far corner of the second field, climb the stile and bear left down the hill. The terraced path leads gradually to a stile giving access to the road. Turn right and follow the road. After a while the road bends sharply to the left and leads down to the farm at Ravensclough.

8. Just before the farm buildings, climb a stile at the end of the wall on the right and go diagonally across a small paddock and over a stile into Ravensclough Wood. The path descends through the wood to a footbridge over the stream and over a stile into a field on the valley floor. The path is straight ahead across the water meadow, between the river on the left and the wooded bank on the right. After 350 metres climb a slight bank above the tree-lined water course on the left. The path comes close to a fence on the left. Follow it down to the corner of the field, cross a stile and go over a stone slab footbridge. Cross the field and climb onto the embankment of the disused railway and turn right. Leave the railway at the former level crossing in front of the station house at Rushton and pass the station on your right, to follow a track down to the picnic area where the walk started.

Walk 2: Rudyard and Denford

John Scott, Sandwell Group

Starting point: Grid Reference SJ 955579, Rudyard Lake car park at the site of the former railway station. Access is signposted at the side of the former railway bridge on the B5331 road which leads from the A523 Leek – Macclesfield road.

Distance: 10 miles (16 kilometres)

Useful maps: Ordnance Survey Outdoor Leisure 24 The Peak District White Peak Area, or Ordnance Survey Pathfinder 792 Kidsgrove and Leek, or Ordnance Survey Landranger 118 Stoke-on-Trent and Macclesfield.

Terrain: Mostly level but including some modest slopes

---

1. Return down the ramp to the B5331 road. Take care as cars may be turning up the ramp from the road to use the car park. Turn left and walk along the pavement. Just before the speed restriction sign turn left down the stepped ramp to join the Staffordshire Way as it follows the canal feeder channel.

   Rudyard reservoir and the canal feeder were constructed in 1831 to supply water to the Caldon Canal whose extension to Uttoxeter had been completed twenty years earlier.

   Continue to follow the Staffordshire Way along the left bank of the canal feeder for a distance of approximately 2½ miles (4 kilometres). Shortly after passing a golf course on the left and Ladderedge Country Park on the right, the Staffordshire Way meets the main A53, Stoke-on-Trent – Leek road. This is where the walk leaves the Staffordshire Way.

2. Cross the road to a cattle grid directly opposite. Go over the cattle grid and follow the tarmac track for approximately 100

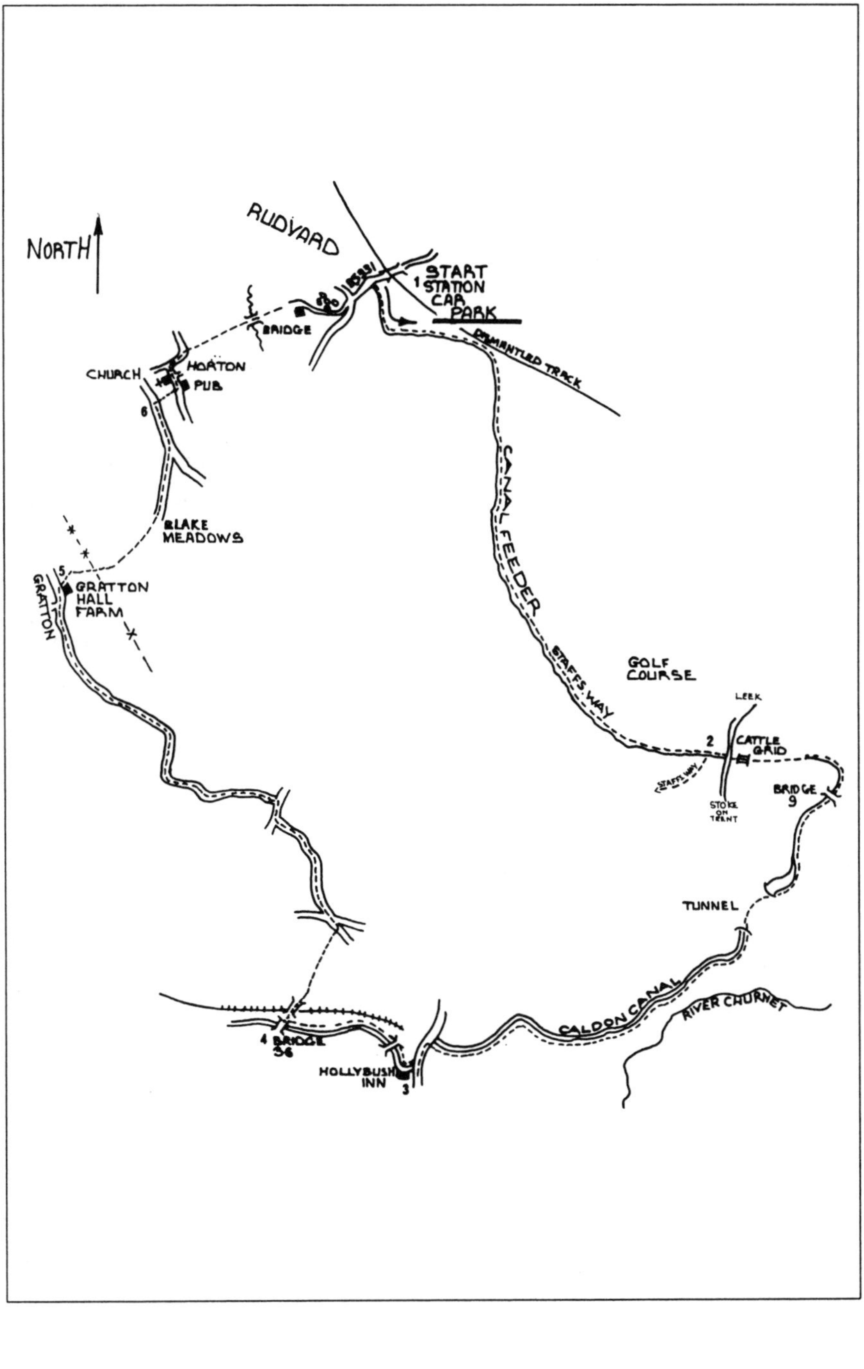
NORTH
RUDYARD
1 START STATION CAR PARK
BRIDGE
DISMANTLED TRACK
CHURCH
HORTON
PUB
6
BLAKE MEADOWS
5
GRATTON
GRATTON HALL FARM
CANAL FEEDER
STAFFS WAY
GOLF COURSE
LEEK
2
CATTLE GRID
STAFFS WAY
STOKE ON TRENT
BRIDGE 9
TUNNEL
CALDON CANAL
RIVER CHURNET
4 BRIDGE 36
HOLLYBUSH INN
3

metres. Just before a concrete bridge, turn left onto a grassy path to regain the feeder channel.

This section of the walk follows the red waymarks of a route from Deep Hayes Country Park. Deep Hayes Country Park was formed by an agreement between Severn Trent Water, Staffordshire County Council, Staffordshire Moorlands District Council, and the Countryside Commission in 1979. The Park offers a choice of three waymarked circular routes, red, blue, and green, passing through a variety of attractive landscapes, unique to Staffordshire.

After approximately 200 metres, the feeder channel goes underground. Follow the field path with the river Churnet on the left until the feeder channel re-appears only to end abruptly as it discharges into the end of the Leek arm of the Caldon Canal. On approaching the river bridge, turn right through a gap at the side of a gate to gain access to the towpath. Follow the towpath with the canal on the right. After bridge number 9, the canal enters a tunnel and the towpath is diverted over the hill. Follow the clear gravel path through a series of stiles and then down some steps to rejoin the canal at a wide turning area.

By backtracking a short way along the towpath, a close-up view of the splendid portal to the tunnel can be obtained. A plaque commemorates the re-opening to navigation in 1983 following extensive repair work.

This stretch of towpath is particularly scenic. After the tall and ornate tower of St Edward's Hospital on the left, the path meanders along the contours of the valley, eventually passing bridges number 7 and 6 with some impressive gardens leading down to the canal on the far side. The red waymarked route leaves our circuit at bridge 6 (Horse Bridge). Shortly beyond Horse Bridge an overflow channel leads into the back garden of a cottage. Boat moorings on the right precede bridges number 5 and 4.

Continue along the towpath as far as bridge number 4.

3. Walk under the bridge and then turn left to leave the towpath and join a road. Turn right and follow the road over the bridge of the disused railway to gain access to the car park of the Hollybush Inn.

This attractive canal-side inn is at the mid-point of the walk and provides bar meals. There is also a picturesque area by the side of the canal to enjoy a picnic stop. The canal at the side of the inn is the Caldon Canal. The 17½ mile section of the canal between Etruria and Froghall dates from 1779 and the extension to Uttoxeter was completed in 1811. The canal was used by the Wedgwood factory at Etruria and to carry limestone from the Caldon Low quarries near Froghall. Nearby is the Hazlehurst Aqueduct which was built in 1841 to take the

The Hollybush Inn

Leek Arm over the original canal. At the junction of the Leek Arm and the main canal there are three locks to raise the water level and a superb cast iron footbridge, made in 1849, connecting the two towpaths.

Continue along the towpath of the Caldon Canal with the water on the left. Pass under bridges 37 and 36.

4. Immediately after bridge number 36 and to the right of the first cottage, cross a stile and follow the path downhill to a gate. Go through the gate and cross the disused railway. Turn right on leaving the track-bed to cross a brook via a footbridge. Take the footpath straight ahead for forty metres to a wooden footbridge and stiles in the hedge on the left. Cross the bridge and go up the hill with the hedge on the right crossing two fields and two stiles to reach a bungalow. The public footpath enters the garden of the bungalow via a stile and leaves by another stile that is hidden behind a fir tree in the right corner. Turn left in the lane and in a few metres, cross the main road and enter Honeysuckle Lane. Walk to the far end of Honeysuckle Lane and turn right. After 100 metres, turn left along the lane signposted to Gratton. Follow this lane for 1¼ miles (2 kilometres) to Gratton Hall Farm, on the right hand side of the road.

5. Just past the farm go through a wooden gate on the right and walk along a short track. At the end of the track, turn left and go over a stone step stile. Go forward initially and then right to walk down the field keeping the hedge on the left. Walk between the hedge and a pylon and just before the field corner pass between two metal posts in the hedge on the left. Cross the field diagonally to the right heading towards a farmhouse partly hidden behind trees, and go through a metal gate in the field corner. Continue in the same direction to a stile with stone pillars. Cross the stile and follow the hedge on the left for a few metres to a footbridge over a brook. Cross the footbridge and go through a gate on the right of the farmhouse and enter a small enclosure. Leave the enclosure via another gate giving access to the farm drive.

Follow the drive away from the house going up a slight slope and with the hedge on the right. Pass through a metal gate with stone pillars and then turn left through another metal gate to leave the drive and enter a narrow field. Go diagonally right across the field to a stile on the left of a large oak. Cross the stile and continue in the same direction to the corner of the field where there is a gate giving access to a lane. Turn left and walk along the lane for 300 metres to a finger post and a stile in the hedge on the right opposite Toll Gate Cottage. Cross the field keeping parallel with the stone wall on the left to reach a stone step stile and a finger post near to the Crown Public House in Horton.

6. Walk past the public house and the lych-gate of the church to reach a T-junction. Turn right and follow the sunken lane for 150 metres until it bends sharply to the left. Do not turn left but go straight ahead through a small wooden gate. Follow the power-line up the hill to reach a stile in a stone wall just to the left of a power-line pole. Cross the stile and continue in the same direction to the corner of a stone wall. Follow the wall, keeping it on the right. Cross a stone footbridge and a stile and continue up the field with the wall on the right. Just before the farm go through a stone stile on the right and almost immediately through another giving access to a farm track. Turn right and follow the farm track through woods to the road. Turn right to reach the Poachers Tavern and the B5331. Follow the B5331 downhill to the left to return to the car park at the start of the walk.

Walk 3: Deep Hayes

Andrew Trimmings, Stone Group

Starting point: Grid Reference SJ 961535, Deep Hayes Country Park which is situated 2 miles south west of Leek. The easiest approach is from the north and this is recommended. Turn off the A53 Leek – Hanley road, at Longsdon and follow the brown signs. The alternative approach from the east, uses very narrow lanes and is not recommended.

Distance: 10 miles (16 kilometres)

Useful maps: Ordnance Survey Outdoor Leisure 24 The Peak District White Peak Area, or Ordnance Survey Pathfinder 792 Kidsgrove and Leek, or Ordnance Survey Landranger 118 Stoke-on-Trent and Macclesfield.

Terrain: The walk begins with easy towpath walking before a gentle ascent and descent to the village of Stanley. Another gentle ascent to the halfway point is followed by a descent to the Caldon Canal where the route rejoins the towpath and follows the Staffordshire Way back to Deep Hayes. There are breathtaking views at several points on the walk.

Deep Hayes Country Park is 143 acres of woods, meadows and pools that provide an opportunity to explore some of North Staffordshire's lovely countryside. The pools were constructed in the middle of the last century to replenish the River Churnet with water lost in serving local mills. There are toilets and a visitor centre adjacent to the car park.

1. Return to the vehicle entrance on Park Lane and turn left to cross the canal bridge. Turn immediately right and descend over the stile to the towpath. Walk under the bridge and follow the towpath. Go under bridge number 38 passing the Hollybush Inn and a row of terraced houses. The towpath turns 90 degrees to the right before coming to Hazlehurst aqueduct.

Bridge No. 3

2. Immediately before the aqueduct, climb the steps on the right to reach the Leek arm of the canal. Cross bridge number 3 and continue along the towpath, with the water on the left, past Hazlehurst moorings (spelt *Hazelhurst* on the notice board).

At bridge number 2, the main arm of the canal is to the right and Hazelhurst Locks are prominent.

Just before bridge number 1, cross the stile at the right of the bridge and turn left to cross bridge number 1.

Much of this walk, but not all of it, follows the green arrows of a circuit from Deep Hayes Country Park; take care not to be misled by the green arrows.

In 1772 James Brindley was asked to survey the route of a possible canal from the Trent & Mersey to Caldon Low quarries. Reputedly, he caught a cold during the survey and died shortly afterwards. However, by 1778 the Caldon Canal was complete,

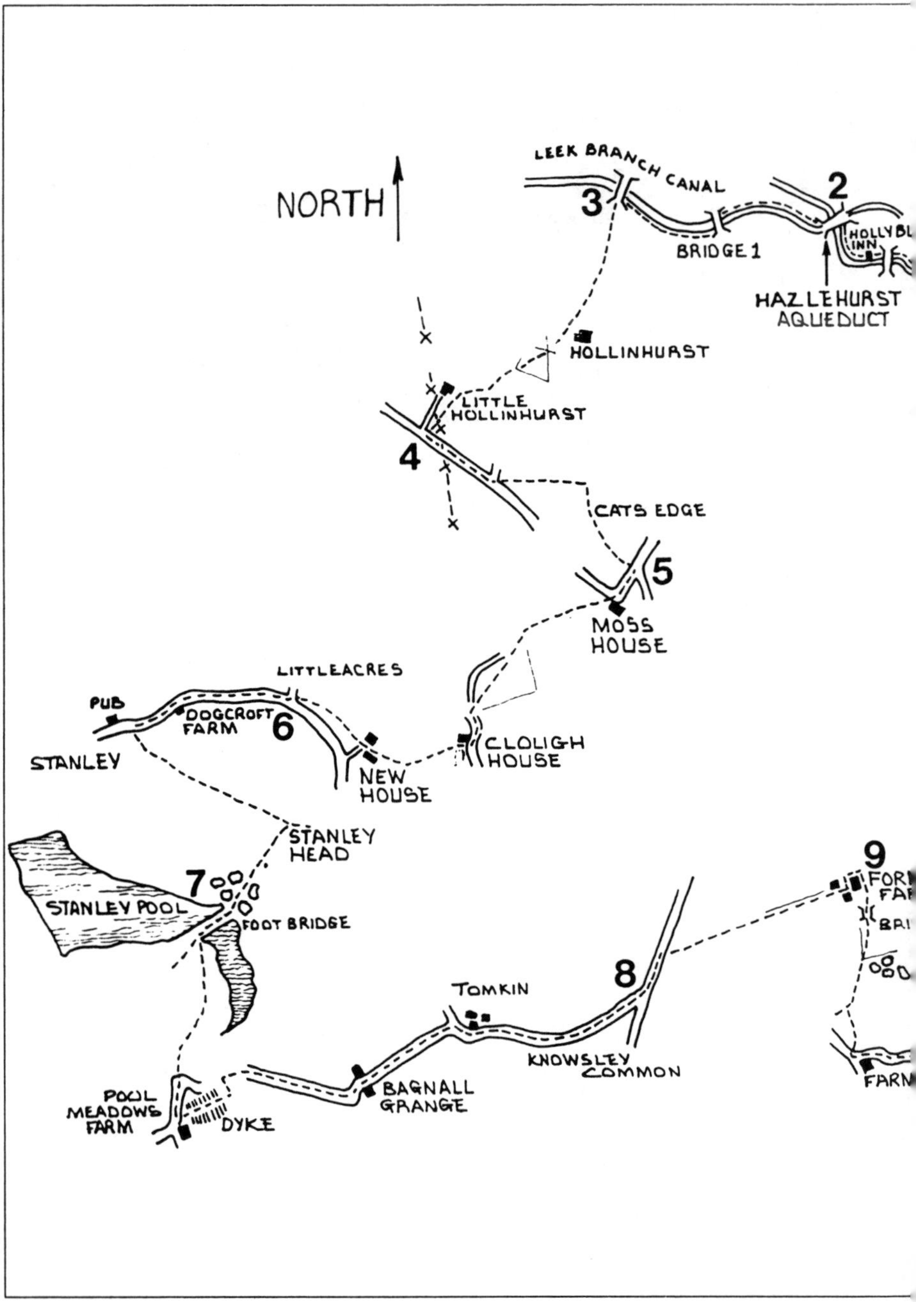
NORTH
LEEK BRANCH CANAL
3
2
BRIDGE 1
HOLLYBU
INN
HAZLEHURST
AQUEDUCT
HOLLINHURST
LITTLE
HOLLINHURST
4
CATS EDGE
5
MOSS
HOUSE
LITTLEACRES
PUB
DOGCROFT
FARM
6
STANLEY
CLOUGH
HOUSE
NEW
HOUSE
STANLEY
HEAD
7
STANLEY POOL
FOOT BRIDGE
9
TOMKIN
8
KNOWSLEY
COMMON
BAGNALL
GRANGE
POOL
MEADOWS
FARM
DYKE

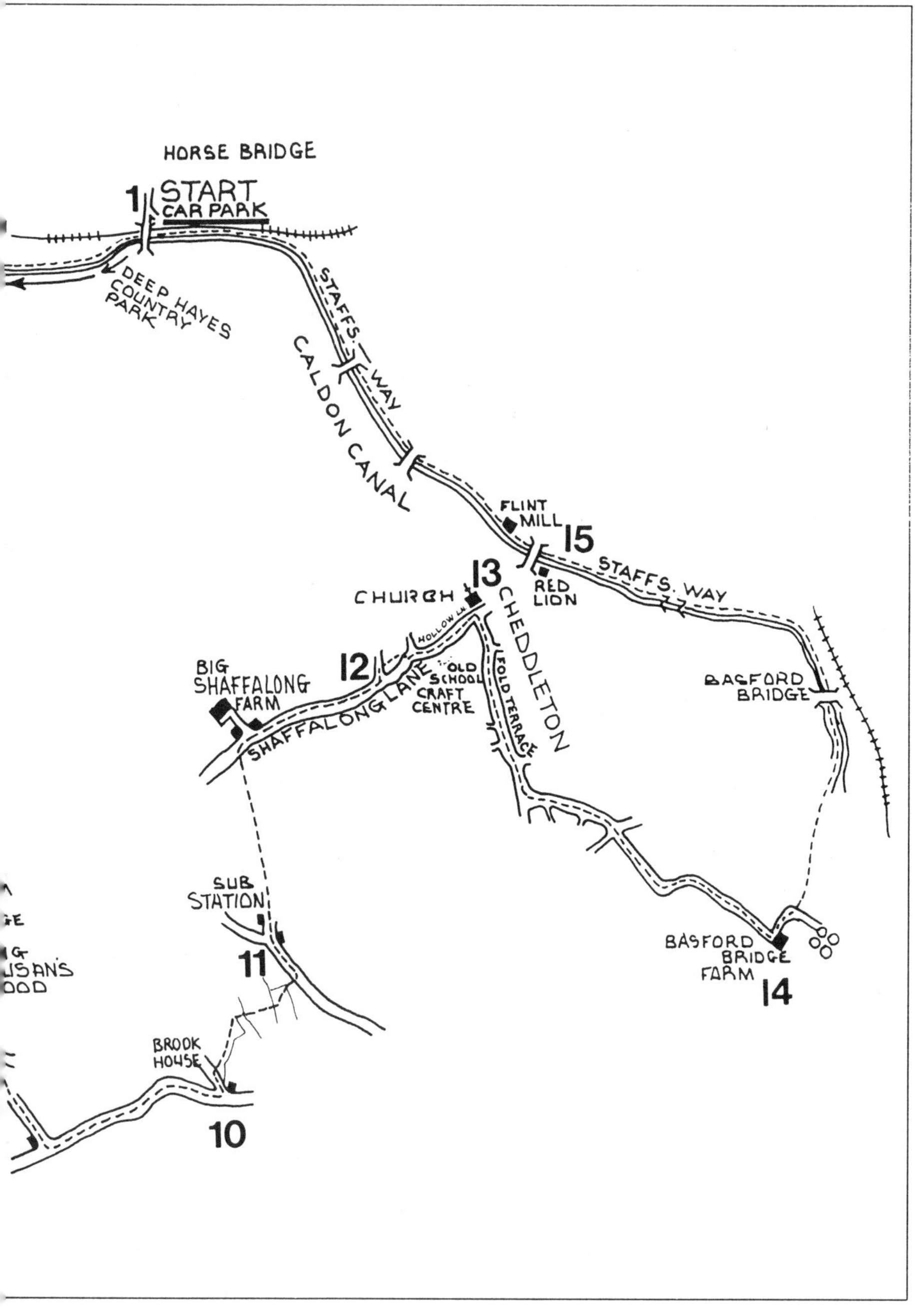
HORSE BRIDGE
1
START
CAR PARK
DEEP HAYES COUNTRY PARK
STAFFS. WAY
CALDON CANAL
FLINT MILL
15
RED LION
STAFFS. WAY
13
CHURCH
CHEDDLETON
HOLLOW LN
12
BIG SHAFFALONG FARM
SHAFFALONG LANE
OLD SCHOOL CRAFT CENTRE
FOLD TERRACE
BASFORD BRIDGE
SUB STATION
11
BASFORD BRIDGE FARM
14
BROOK HOUSE
10

and in 1801 the Leek feeder arm became operational, linking the Caldon Canal to the new reservoir at Rudyard. The original line, with three locks, was replaced by "New Hazelhurst Locks" and the aqueduct in 1841.

3. Cross the stile at the far side of the bridge. Walk up the slope in the direction of some farm buildings, to a gate in the stone wall at the top right hand corner of the field. Pass through the gate and head towards the right hand side of the farm buildings. A few metres from the barn, cross a stile and walk diagonally left to the next stile two-thirds of the way up the opposite boundary. Cross the next field, heading just to the left of an electricity pylon to find a stile hidden in the hedge. Cross the stile and walk diagonally across the field, heading mid-way between the electricity pylons to a stile obscured by a holly bush. Cross this stile and continue in the same direction to a stone squeeze stile modified by a wooden stile behind it.

Here, there is a splendid view to the right of the radio station at Croker Hill, Bosley.

Pass to the left of the bungalow and follow the fence on the right boundary of the field to a stile in the far corner.

4. At the road, turn left and walk up the hill for 300 metres. Turn left into the entrance to Hollinhurst Farm. Do not walk along the farm drive but turn right immediately and cross a narrow stile. Keeping to the boundary on the right cross two fields to a stile in the far corner of the second field.

This is Cats Edge which provides spectacular views on all sides. To the West are the Cheshire Plain, Shropshire and Wales. To the North-east are the Roaches with Hen Cloud to the right, and the Vale of Trent lying to the South.

Cross the stile and turn right. Follow the wall to the corner of the field where there is a stone stile. Cross the stile and continue in the same direction, initially with a wall on the left, to the next stile and cross it to gain access to the road. Turn right and walk 100 metres downhill to where the road bends sharply to the right.

5. Do not turn right but continue ahead to cross the stone stile at the side of a gate. Walk down the field, keeping the hedge on the left, to the field corner, where there are two gateways. Go through the gateway on the left and then immediately go through another gateway. Walk diagonally across the field in the direction of some farm buildings, to the far corner of the field where there is a gate. Pass through the gate and follow the grassy track to Clough House. Turn left to walk down the drive. After a few paces, at a three-way footpath sign, turn right and walk at the side of the fence at the rear of the farm garden, to a gate in the corner of the field. Go through the gate and turn right to walk across the corner of the field to a stone squeeze stile with a wooden stile behind it.

Cross the stile and follow the left boundary of the field to reach a stile in the cross-fence. Cross the ditch into the next field. Cross the field diagonally to the right towards the farm and cross the stile next to a gate. Walk between the farm buildings and after 50 metres, where the farm track turns left, continue straight on through a wall-stile. Walk past a wooden hut and go through a wooden gap-stile in the hedge. Walk along the field with the stone wall on the right for a few paces until a house on top of a bank can be seen on the left. Walk up to the hedge behind the house and walk with the hedge on the left, to the hedge corner. From the corner, walk diagonally left across the field to a bridle gate near the field corner. Go through the bridle gate and turn left to reach the road by Little Acres Farm.

6. Turn right and follow the road towards the village of Stanley. After 500 metres, just as the road begins to descend and twenty metres before the Travellers' Rest Public House on the right, there is a stone stile on the left. Go through the stile and walk diagonally across the field to a stone stile in the opposite corner. Go over the stile into the next field and turn left. Follow the left boundary of the field to the next stile. Cross the stile and continue in the same direction but now with the field boundary on the right. Keeping the boundary on the right, walk to the far corner of the field where there is a stile next to a gate. Cross the stile and continue, now with the boundary on the left, to the next stile. Go over this stile and, continuing in the same direction, cross the field to two footbridges which form an L-shape. Cross both footbridges and descend gently, with a ditch on the right, through the woods to Stanley Pool. Straight ahead is a long footbridge across the Pool.

Stanley Pool was built in 1783 both as a feeder for the canal system and to provide water for the mills in Stanley that were used for ceramics. A further dam was constructed in 1840 to correspond with the newly cut Leek Branch of the Caldon Canal. Floods in 1927 caused the dam to collapse, but another one was built in 1940. Today, the nearby Stanley Head Outdoor Centre uses Stanley Pool for canoeing and sailing.

7. Walk over the footbridge to a stile on the far side, cross it, and bear left to cross the end of the field to another stile. Continue in the same direction to cross the next stile, and follow the right boundary to a stone stile by a gate. Cross the stile. The path now leaves the right hand boundary hedge and curves gently to the left round the hill side to join a farm track. Follow the track to the left to Pool Meadows Farm. At the entrance to the farmyard, the track turns to the right. Do not follow the track but go over a stile on the left of the entrance and follow the right boundary of the field for 100 metres to a stile on the right. Cross the stile and walk through a narrow avenue of trees along the top of a short dyke. Descend to a footbridge. Cross the footbridge and climb the steps to a stile. Beyond the stile, cross the field and climb some more steps that lead up to a field. Cross this field to a stone squeeze stile. Pass through

A superb cast-iron footbridge on the route of this walk

the stile and turn right to ascend through a narrow gully of trees and bushes. This emerges by a stile that leads on to a farm track.

Behind and to the left, in clear weather, the folly at Mow Cop can be seen in the distance beyond Stanley Pool.

Follow the track. It turns left and passes between the farm buildings and then continues as a tarmac track to the road at Tomkin. At the road, turn right and ascend gently to the picnic area at Knowsley Common with its superb views.

"Tom-kin" takes its name from a gruesome tale dating back to the Civil War. A drummer-boy with King Charles' Cavalier army became separated from the main troop and fell into the hands of Cromwell's Roundheads. The boy's name was Tom and, showing no mercy, they skinned poor Tom alive.

8. At the far side of the common, follow the road round to the left in the direction of Denford. On the right hand side, just beyond the driveway of the first house on the right, there is a stone stile. Go over the stile and cross the field to a stile in the opposite wall. Cross this stile and, continuing in the same direction, descend through a large field to a stile in a stone cross-wall just to the left of a gate. Cross the stile and, with a stone wall on the left, continue towards the farm. Cross a stile at the left of a gate and walk between some cattle sheds to emerge in the farmyard. Ignore the green waymarker pointing to the left and turn right, towards the farmhouse.

9. Go through the gate leading to the front door of the farmhouse and turn left and then right round the farmhouse. Continue through a thicket to a wooden bridge. Beyond the bridge, walk to the stile in the fence opposite. Cross it and go to the stile in the top right hand corner of the field. Go over the stile and cross the field diagonally left to a stile at the side of a gate. Go over the stile. Walk through the field, parallel to the stone wall on the right, to reach a stile next to a gate in a fence just to the right of a farm. Go over the stile to reach a track, cross the track and immediately go over the stile at the side of a gate. Follow the drive for 30 metres to the entrance to the farmyard. Turn left and go over a stile next to a gate. Follow the track downhill through the next gateway. Ignore the track that goes straight ahead, and follow the track sweeping to the right, for 150 metres. After 150 metres, there are two gates, one on each side of the track. Turn through the gate on the right and follow the boundary on the right to another gate. Cross this and continue past a house to a T-junction of tracks. Turn left and follow the track downhill. Ignore a track that slopes up leftwards to the rear of a farm, and continue along the main track which now ascends to meet a concrete farm drive at the top of the slope.

10. Turn left and follow the drive to the entrance of the farmyard. Enter the yard and turn immediately right to cross a stile at the side of a farm gate. Follow the track beside the boundary hedge on the right until the hedge turns sharply to the right. At this point cross the field diagonally left to the right-most gate of two gates in the boundary opposite. Do not go through the gate but cross the wooden stile next to it in the fence on the right and go immediately through a kissing gate. Follow the left boundary hedge to the next kissing gate and go through it. Cross the field diagonally to the left and go over two stiles in a double fence. Turn right and follow the hedge to the corner where a stile gives access to the road. Turn left and follow the road for 150 metres to a left hand bend where, on the right, there is a stile next to a gate.

11. Go over the stile and pass to the right of an electricity sub-station. Continue in the same direction across the field to a fence corner that juts into the field. Keeping the fence on the right, continue to the far corner of the field where there is a stile at the side of a gate giving access to Shaffalong Lane. Cross the stile and turn right to pass Big Shaffalong Farm before descending along the lane. Four hundred metres beyond the farm, there is a track on the left by two horse-chestnut trees. Follow the track for 10 metres and pass through a stone stile on the right. Cross the field to emerge through another stone stile at the Old School Craft Centre.

The Old School was built in 1862 and education continued there until 1986. In the summer of 1995 it opened as a Craft Centre and Tea Room, providing excellent fare (including Sunday lunch) in friendly surroundings. The Craft Centre stocks local goods, and the centre is well worth a visit. There is ample parking to the rear, and the Centre is just a mile away from Deep Hayes Country Park, via Park Lane.

12. Leave the craft centre, cross the road to the pavement on the other side and turn left to walk along Hollow Lane to St Edward's Church.

Built in the 12th century, the church of St Edward the

Confessor lies in a splendid setting, with lovely views from the graveyard to the rear. William Morris designed many of its stained glass windows, some being dedicated to the Powys family from nearby Westwood Manor. It was Thomas Powys who quelled the Pottery riots in 1842 at the time of the Chartist uprisings. The adjacent Black Lion public house lies opposite the remains of the village stocks.

13. Almost opposite the entrance to the church, turn right at the side of a Butcher's shop into Fold Terrace. At the end of the lane, pass to the right of the Vicarage and follow the narrow footpath to a road. Turn left and walk down to the main road. Turn right and walk up the pavement to the zebra crossing. Cross the main road with extreme caution, and walk to the T-junction at the far end of the avenue opposite. Cross the road ahead and follow the tarmac track almost opposite. The track swings sharp left and then sharp right before descending to Basfordbridge Farm.

14. Cross the farmyard and leave it via a concrete track on the left. Several paths meet at this point. Do not descend towards the filter beds but continue along the concrete track for 50 metres. At this point the farm track turns right to go downhill but straight ahead there are two farm gates. Go through the gate on the left and walk down the field keeping to the boundary on the right. Continue to the far corner of the field where there is a locked gate. At the left of the locked gate there is a tree and hidden behind the tree is another gate which is not locked. Pass through the gate and follow the well-defined track downhill.

Rolling stock belonging to the North Staffordshire Railway Company is visible as the Caldon Canal comes into view on the right.

The path swings left to a stile by a gate. Cross the stile and after 100 metres, cross another stile and reach the rear entrance of The Boat Inn. At the junction of the road and the canal, cross the bridge, turn left and descend the steps to join the Staffordshire Way on the towpath. Continue along the towpath with the water on the left. After almost a mile, pass two locks within 100 metres and continue past the Red Lion Public House which is on the opposite side of the canal.

A short distance along the road from The Boat Inn is Cheddleton Railway Station, the home of the North Staffordshire Railway Company. This Jacobean style station of 1849 is one of several built along the Churnet Valley line during the last century, and was saved from demolition in 1974. At present, a short section of the line through a 531-yard tunnel to Leekbrook is operational and "in steam" at weekends. The Churnet Valley Railway has plans to re-open a further 6 miles, initially, taking steam locomotives to Consall Forge.

15. Walk under bridge number 42 carrying the A520, to reach Cheddleton Flint Mill on the other side.

Cheddleton Flint Mill worked commercially as recently as 1963. The Mill is run by The Cheddleton Flint Mill Industrial Heritage Trust, who began to renovate it in 1967. The two large waterwheels, which powered the process of grinding flint, are still operational. The Caldon Canal was used to transport the end product, known as slip, to The Potteries. There is a wide collection of exhibits on display, and entrance is free of charge, though donations are welcome. The Mill is open to the public on Saturday and Sunday afternoons throughout the year, and on most weekdays.

Continue along the towpath. On reaching the steps and stile by the concrete bridge where the walk began, climb up to the road and, leaving the Staffordshire Way, turn left to cross the canal and return to the car park at Deep Hayes.

Walk 4: Weaver Hills and Churnet Valley

Gareth Williams, Walsall Group

Starting point: Grid reference SK 085478. Approaching from Ashbourne on the A52, turn left into the quarry road at Rue Hill. Park in the lay-by on the left just past a telephone box.

Distance: 11 miles (17.5 kilometres)

Useful maps: Ordnance Survey Pathfinder 810 Ashbourne and the Churnet Valley or Ordnance Survey Landranger 119 Buxton, Matlock and Dovedale or Landranger 128 Derby and Burton upon Trent.

Terrain: The walk begins in limestone country by Wardlow quarries in the Weaver Hills and continues through the gentler parklands of Wooton, Alton and Farley. On a clear day it offers a kaleidoscopic multitude of views in an ever changing landscape. But do not be misled; this is the most challenging walk in the book. It has several short steep climbs and descents and requires close attention to the route description. The walk is best done for the first time during late May or early June when the days are long and the vegetation is short. But the walk is full of interest and merits repeating at any time of the year.

---

1. Walk along the road, passing two houses on the left and quarry buildings on the right. The road terminates in a private parking area; continue through this to a gate and small stile on the right. Cross the stile and follow the green track to a gate with a small stile at the side of it. Cross into the field and follow the left hand field boundary towards the next field corner. There is a stile next to a gate in the corner of the field, ignore this stile and cut diagonally across the corner to another stile 75 metres to the right.

2. Go over the stile and take a few steps into the field until,

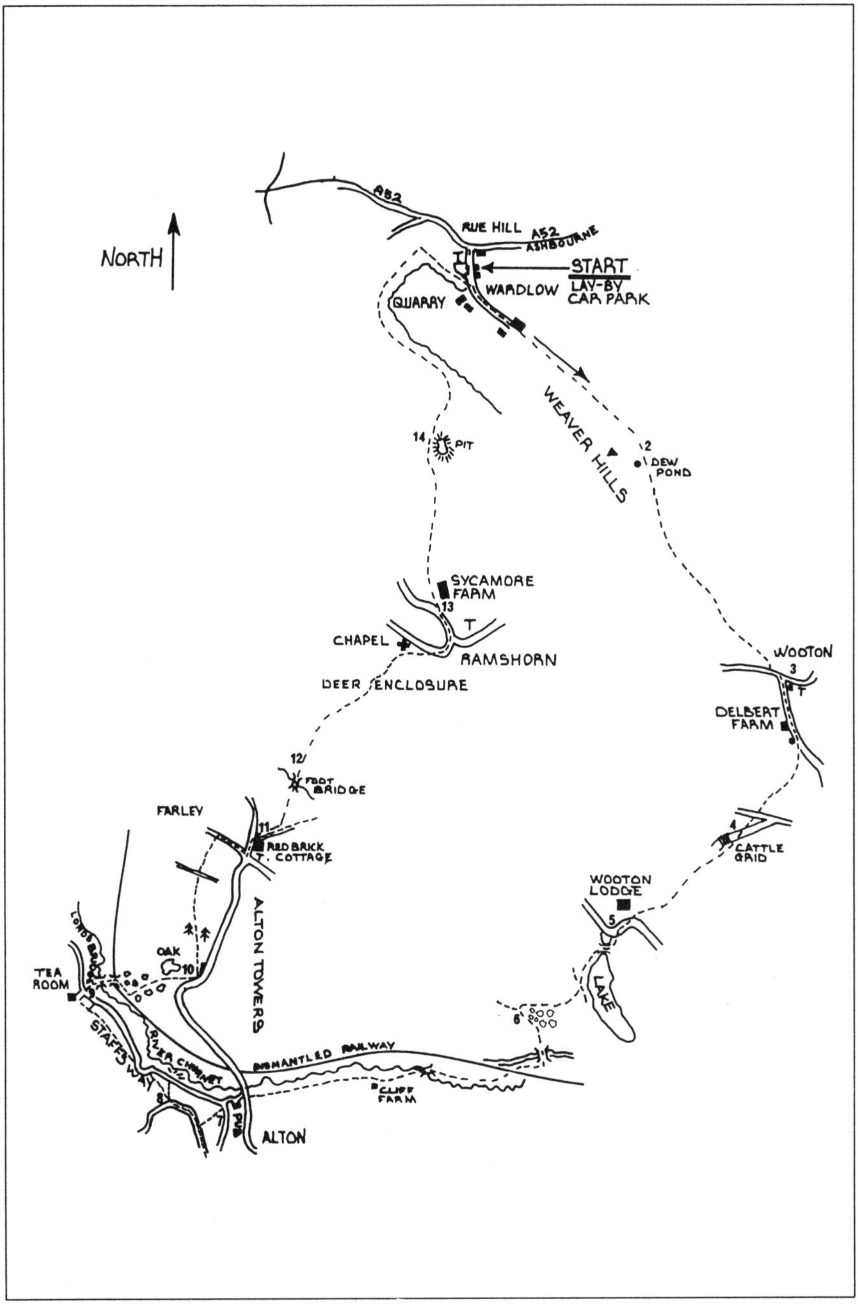
A52
RUE HILL
A52
ASHBOURNE
NORTH
START
LAY-BY
CAR PARK
WARDLOW
QUARRY
WEAVER HILLS
2
DEW POND
14
PIT
SYCAMORE FARM
13
T
CHAPEL
RAMSHORN
DEER ENCLOSURE
WOOTON
3
T
DELBERT FARM
12
FOOT BRIDGE
4
CATTLE GRID
FARLEY
11
T. COTTAGE
WOOTON LODGE
5
LAKE
ALTON TOWERS
OAK
10
TEA ROOM
STAFFS WAY
RIVER CHURNET
DISMANTLED RAILWAY
6
CLIFF FARM
8
PUB
ALTON

diagonally across to the right, a dew pond, and just beyond it, the corner of a wall that juts into the field can be seen.

A dew pond is a small, man-made depression, traditionally lined with clay, which collects water to provide drink for sheep and cattle in high dry areas. Very little of the water comes from dew, most is derived from rain.

From this corner there is a choice of paths. The following description traces the definitive route. The alternative, which is signposted and forms part of an East Staffordshire Leisure Services walk, crosses the fence slightly higher up the hill before descending more steeply to the metal gate in the wall below.

Walk to this corner and continue in the same direction towards the fence ahead. Go over the stile. Do not follow the wall on the right; it descends down the slope and turns left. Instead, walk round the contour of the hill keeping at the same level until the wall can again be seen below. Continue round the hill until a metal gate can be seen in this same wall. Descend to the gate. Go through the gate or cross the diminutive ladder stile at the side and then go immediately through a gap in the very dilapidated wall on the left. Facing across the slope, a large and ancient apple tree can be seen on the other side of the field just where the slope on the left starts to level out. Fifty metres to the right of this tree there is a stile in the field boundary. Cross the field to the stile and go over it into the next field. Walk diagonally right to the field corner where there is a track. Follow the track to the right past a cricket field to reach a road.

3. Turn left and walk into the hamlet of Wooton. At the first junction, turn right to pass between Toll Gate House on the right and Toll Gate Cottage on the left. Pass Delbert Farm at the bottom of the hill and just past the next cottage on the right, go through a galvanised gate and follow the track rising to the left. Where the track opens into a field, a dry stone wall can be seen to start in the middle of the field just to the right of some tall trees. Cross to the wall and keeping it on the right, follow it until it turns right. Here continue forward to a stile over a fence. Cross the stile and turn right to find a high ladder stile that might be hidden by branches at the base of a tree. Climb the stile and follow the path diagonally left, down through the wooded area. Climb a stile over deer fencing and cross a descending track at the point where it becomes metalled. Walk down the grassy slope following the fence to a road. Cross this road and walk diagonally right to reach a second road.

4. Follow the road to the right, but shortly before reaching a cattle grid, go diagonally left and pick up a stone wall and a deer fence on the right. The fence runs parallel to the road. Follow the fence to a tall kissing gate. Go through the gate, turn left and follow the path through the shrubs. On emerging from the rhododendrons keep a fenced beech hedge on the left for a few metres and then bear right to pass to the right of some buildings.

The Hall on the right is Wootton Lodge, built at the end of the sixteenth or the beginning of the seventeenth century and now occupied by the Bamfords who build JCB earth moving machinery at Rocester. The lake, terraces and large-scale rockeries demonstrate the effectiveness of their machines.

On reaching a road, walk straight over it and cross grassland towards conifer trees, bearing right between two stretches of ranch type fencing that narrow to a path. The path leads to a wooden door that gives access, via a very unusual walled path, to a road.

Adventurous young children will enjoy finding this secret door and the passage beyond but ensure that any energetic youngsters wait for their less energetic adult companions to catch up before going through this gate. It leads to a very narrow passage between walls and the passage ends abruptly at a road. Well-built adults might find the narrow passage to be more of an obstruction than an exit. In earlier times the designers of this passage could have found expression for their undoubted skills in the design of defence systems for Norman castles.

5. Turn right and on reaching a right hand bend, leave the road and go through a concealed gap in the wall ahead. Turn left to a road. Go right, over a small bridge and then almost immediately left on a descending path with the lake on the left. Follow the lake towards a T-junction where there is a large boulder on the left. Just before the boulder, turn right to a rising path through the woods. Emerging from the woods, turn right and follow the way-marked path through the grass to a track. Cross the track to reach a stile. Climb the stile and follow the fence on the right to arrive at a stile on the left. Cross this and walk diagonally right to the woods where, at a junction of paths, continue directly ahead to a wooden stile which is at the side of an old stone squeezer stile. Cross the wooden stile.

6. Approximately 25 metres from the wooden stile there is a track. Turn right onto the track and follow it round to the left to meet, after a further 40 metres, another track. Follow this to the left and after a further 50 metres, turn off to the left along a narrow descending path. Go over a wooden stile and continue down to a wooden gate giving access to an old stone bridge. Cross the bridge and turn immediately right to a stile. Cross the stile and follow the path to reach the track-bed of the former Churnet railway. Cross the track-bed to a gate and head diagonally right to the bank of the river Churnet. Follow the river up stream. Cross it at the second footbridge and take a rising path to the right just above the river. On reaching a track near the entrance gate to Cliff Farm, turn right and follow the track to a road. Cross the road and the Talbot public house will be "discovered" on the left.

7. In the gap between the Talbot and the Alton Bridge Hotel, there is a narrow walled path. Follow the path and at the road turn right and then almost immediately turn left through low squeezer stones and take a rising path to the left through the bracken and trees. At a cottage, cross a stone wall between the cottage and an outbuilding. Walk through the property and out through the wrought iron gate onto a track. The Staffordshire Way passes along this track.

8. Turn right and at the junction of three paths turn right again. Ignore for the time being the squeezer stile at the side of a gate on the left and go carefully forward to the viewpoint at Toothill Rock.

There is a magnificent view out over the Churnet valley towards Alton Towers theme park. The river can just be seen below, and beyond that, the track-bed of the Churnet railway. Below and to the right, adjacent to the railway can be seen the buildings of the Italianate former railway station. This area has been called "Staffordshire's Rhineland".

Return to the squeezer stile at the side of the gate and turn right. Descend right to a stile and continue down through woodland past sandstone crags on the left to meet a road on a hairpin bend. Follow the bend clockwise for approximately 30 metres and then take a track on the left with a sign for Dimmings Dale, passing a sandstone cottage on the right. After a short distance, at a junction where the main track turns sharply to the left, go straight ahead and after a further 200 metres, leave the track and take a descending path on the right. This soon becomes a sunken track which leads to the Forestry Commission's Dimmings Dale car park and a tea room.

9. Leaving the Staffordshire Way, cross over the road on the right and go through a gate, then over Lord's Bridge spanning the River Churnet, and a second bridge over the former railway.

The water that lies below this bridge is the remains of a contour canal between Froghall and Uttoxeter that was obliterated when the railway was built.

The path bears round to the right and where it divides go left uphill through the woods.

This valley is known as Barbary Gutter. Part-way up, note the steps leading up to the Chained Oak – a large oak tree with

The view from Toothill Rock

some of the branches supported by chains. There are several legends associated with this tree. One legend has it that this place is haunted if you pass by at midnight, another is that the Earl of Shrewsbury had the branches secured to avoid a gypsy's curse, threatening that whenever a branch fell to the ground, one of the Earl's family would die. More prosaically, it is believed to be a remnant of a former ornamental landscape.

Carry on until a lodge is reached by the road.

10. Do not go onto the road but turn left for a few paces along the driveway and then take a signed footpath on the right by way of a stile next to a gate. Cross to another stile and, on rising ground, make for the left of a right hand group of pines and go down to another stile. The path passes through a metal gate to the left of a large pine tree and continues uphill with a metal fence on the right. Pass through a metal gate and cross a farm track to a stile on the left. Ignore the finger post pointing left and go directly across the meadow, heading just to the right of a house whose garden projects into the meadow. Cross a stile at the far side to reach the road near Farley Hall. Turn right following the road and take the first road on the left by Farley Cottage.

11. Just past a red brick cottage on the right, turn right down an old holloway (track) and shortly climb a flight of stone steps on the left and go over a stile. In the middle of the field there is an isolated mature oak tree. Pass between this tree and an old, tall hawthorn hedge and continue downhill to a gate in a metal fence. Go left through the gate and descend and after a few paces cross a footbridge on the right behind an old oak tree.

12. Cross the road and ascend between two metal fences staying with the right hand fence. Follow the fence to the top of the field and turn left still following the fence. Pass a gate in the fence and shortly afterwards go over a stile on the right. Turn left and follow a path for approximately 300 metres to a small wooden footbridge, cross this and follow the path which turns to the right to arrive at a stile. Cross the stile and going a little leftward, walk up through the plantation to a gate in the deer enclosure. Go through this and continue to similar gates just in front of the buildings on the far side. Go through these gates and pass through an iron barred gate on the left. Turn right and then left between two farm buildings, go through another gate and follow the fence on your left to a road, passing a chapel on your left. Turn right to follow the road to Ramshorn and at the first road junction turn left towards Leek.

13. After approximately 200 metres, leave the road and follow the driveway of Sycamore Farm which is on the right. The farm can be identified by the three mature sycamores at the side of the road fronting the farm buildings. Keeping to the left of the buildings, go through a squeezer stile and a gate directly ahead. Follow the descending right hand field boundary to a stile in the field corner. After crossing the stile follow the left hand field boundary and go through a squeezer stile in the first field corner. Cross diagonally right to another squeezer stile and go through it. Follow the ascending right hand field boundary.

14. After passing to the left of the pit at the top of the rise, walk diagonally left until you come to a track on the left hand boundary of the field. Follow the boundary to a double gate in the fence on the left. Pass through the gate and go ahead through a gateway in a dry stone wall. Turn right to a stile and then cross another field to an old gate near a large notice indicating shot firing times. Ascend the path, tending to the left and following marker posts, to a stile. Cross the stile and after rising to the right, contour clockwise around the quarry perimeter fence to a metal gate and track. Turn right to return to the starting point.

Walk 5: Churnet Valley and Dimmings Dale

Jim Allkins, Walsall Group

Starting point: Grid Reference SK 053447, the car park and picnic site by the river Churnet where it is crossed by the B5417 in Oakamoor.

Distance: 10 miles (16 kilometres)

Useful maps: Ordnance Survey Pathfinder 810 Ashbourne and the Churnet Valley or Ordnance Survey Landranger 119 Buxton, Matlock and Dovedale or Landranger 128 Derby and Burton upon Trent.

Terrain: An undulating walk with two short steep climbs.

---

1. From the car park turn left to walk along the road, and accompanied by the River Churnet, take the left turn at the road junction. After approximately 100 metres and on approaching a high stone wall, take the track on the right going uphill through the woods. Crossing over broad forestry tracks continue straight uphill and when nearing the top, follow the path as it veers to the right of a cottage, and go through a gate in the wall ahead. Turn right along a path enclosed between two stone walls then pass over a cattle grid to turn right onto the Staffordshire Way. The surface soon changes to tarmac and continues in the same direction to the T-junction at the end of the lane. At the junction turn right, downhill, to arrive at the footpath to Hawkesmoor on the left. Follow this, uphill, ignoring any tracks off, and the Staffordshire Way signs will lead to the B5417 road.

2. Turn left for a few metres before passing through the impressive gateway on the right.

This gateway was erected in 1933 in memory of John Richard

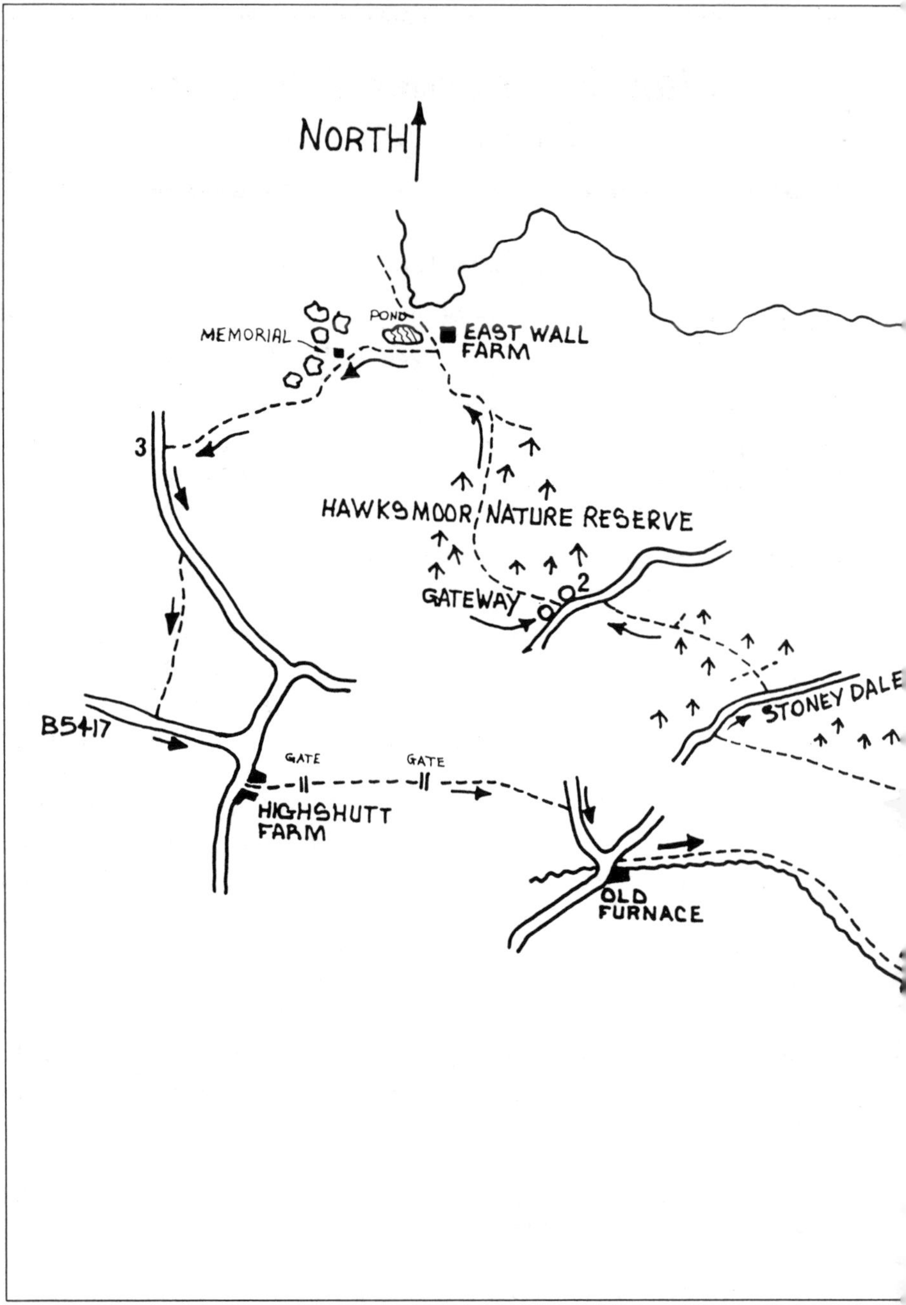
NORTH
POND
MEMORIAL
EAST WALL FARM
3
HAWKSMOOR NATURE RESERVE
GATEWAY
2
STONEY DALE
B5417
GATE
GATE
HIGHSHUTT FARM
OLD FURNACE

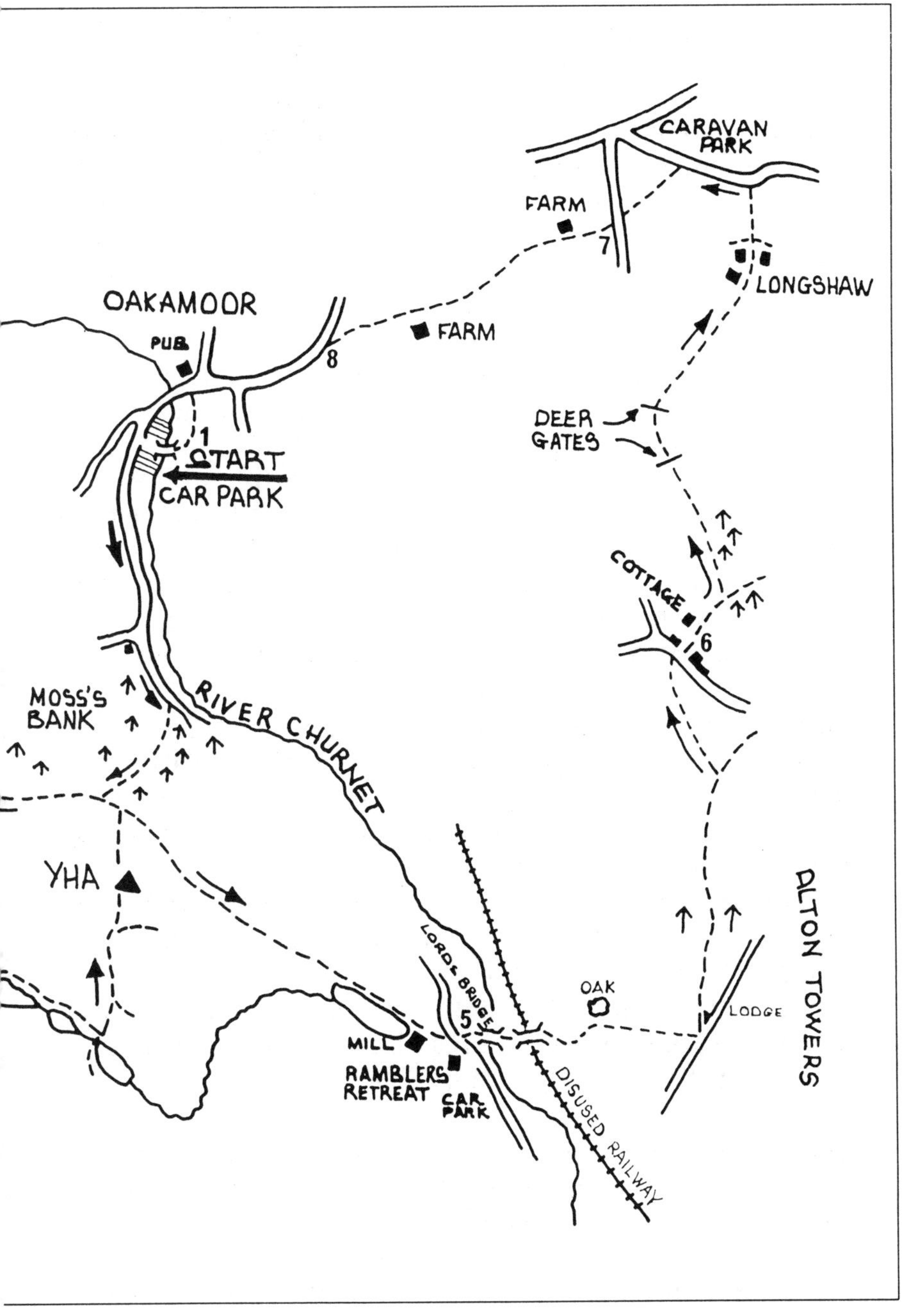
CARAVAN PARK
FARM
7
LONGSHAW
OAKAMOOR
PUB
8
FARM
DEER GATES
1
START
CAR PARK
COTTAGE
6
MOSS'S BANK
RIVER CHURNET
YHA
ALTON TOWERS
LORDS BRIDGE
OAK
LODGE
5
MILL
RAMBLERS RETREAT
CAR PARK
DISUSED RAILWAY

Beech Masefield, the founder of the Hawkesmoor Nature Reserve.

Follow the Staffordshire Way signs downhill. Ignore a broad track joining from the right, and at a fork, go left to cross a stile at the side of a gate. Follow a low brick wall round a corner to the right and then walk at the side of a wooden fence with East Wall Farm to the right. Continue down to the corner of the fence where there is a stile. The Staffordshire Way continues down the valley past a lovely little pond. However do not climb the stile but go left alongside the fence. Keep the fence and the hedge on the right and proceed uphill. Ignore the stile on the right into Gibridding Wood, and after passing a memorial to Major General W. Reid Martin, who we are informed died on this spot in 1892, take the stile on the right beside a metal gate. With the hedge still on the right, follow the green track and on passing a small stream, turn sharp right and then double back left uphill. Go through a gap in the hedge and then straight on to a signpost and stile ahead.

3. Turn left to follow the road. After approximately ¼ mile (400 metres), look out for a footpath sign on the right. Walk across the field keeping the fence to the right, and on reaching the B5417 road, turn left. Where the road swings sharp left, take the road on the right. Enter the yard of Highshutt Farm on the left and continue downhill passing through two gates. Stay on this track where it veers left away from the hedge, then descend to a gate at the bottom of the valley. The path continues with the hedge on the right to reach a lane by way of a stile. Turn downhill to a road junction at Old Furnace to take the bridleway to Dimmings Dale.

4. The path continues downhill and at a vehicle barrier a waymark indicates that the bridleway keeps to the right by the stream. There now follows a series of large ponds.

The ponds form part of a site of Special Scientific Interest running through Dimmings Dale and were originally made to provide water to power the iron mills and later, the corn mills that replaced them.

On reaching a picnic table near to where a broad path crosses the ponds, turn left up the steep steps and at the top turn left again to follow a wide track for a short distance to a way-marked narrow path on the left. Follow the narrow path which cuts across the hill towards the wall. Carry on uphill to pass through a kissing gate.

Here, where there is a memorial plaque to Paul Rey, affords good views down this lovely dale.

Continue straight ahead along the path which follows the line of the left hand wall to another gate leading to Dimmings Dale Youth Hostel. Keep on the same heading past the buildings and just before a cattle grid, turn right down the track to rejoin the Staffordshire Way. At a crossing path carry straight ahead downhill, and after a vehicle barrier, pass the beautifully restored property of Earls Rock. Continuing on, the building on the right is the former Smelting Mill.

The mill was built around 1741 but by 1786 ore smelting had finished and the building was converted into a corn mill.

The next building to appear is the Ramblers Retreat where once again we leave the Staffordshire Way.

Originally one of the lodges to Alton Towers, the Ramblers Retreat was bought, derelict, by the present owners, Gary and Margaret Keeling, in 1978. With much of the rebuilding and refurbishment completed by themselves, it opened in 1981 to provide refreshments for walkers in the area. It is now a licensed restaurant where a friendly welcome awaits all.

5. On reaching the road cross over and go through a gate, then

The Round House, Dimmings Dale

over Lord's Bridge, spanning the River Churnet, and a second bridge over the former railway.

The water that lies below this bridge is the remains of a contour canal between Froghall and Uttoxeter that was obliterated when the railway was built.

The path bears round to the right and where it divides go left uphill through the woods.

This valley is known as Barbary Gutter. Part way up, note the steps leading up to the variously named Chained Oak or Druid's Oak- a large oak tree with some of the branches supported by chains. There are several legends associated with this tree. One legend has it that this place is haunted if you pass by at midnight, another is that the Earl of Shrewsbury had the branches secured to avoid a gypsy's curse, threatening that whenever a branch fell to the ground, one of the Earl's family would die. More prosaically, it is believed to be a remnant of a former ornamental landscape.

Carry on until a lodge is reached by the road. Do not go onto the road but turn left for a few paces along the driveway and then take a footpath on the right by way of a stile next to a gate.

Near here you can see, over to the right, peeping through the trees, some of the theme park rides of Alton Towers.

Cross to another stile and, on rising ground, make for the left of a right hand group of pines and go down to another stile. The path passes through a metal gate to the left of a large pine tree and continues up hill with a metal fence on the right. Pass through a metal gate and cross a farm track to a stile on the left. Over the stile take the path waymarked to the left, heading in the direction of a white farm building. The next stile is just to the right of this building. Go over the stile, cross a drive, go over the next stile and through a squeezer stile to the lane.

6. Go up the lane, almost opposite, past Cliffe Cottage. The public footpath continues up the road. Where the tarmac finishes, continue ahead through a squeeze stile and through a narrow gap in the deer fence. Cross the drive, go through another fence gap and turn sharp left before a stile. Do not go over it. Keep to the main track through the woods, where the fence on the left is never far away. Pass through a gate in the deer fence and carry on along the same heading. The remains of an old squeezer stile indicates the way to a 'step-gate' in the electrified fence. A waymark on a telegraph pole shows the direction to take. Keep in this general direction and as the brow of the hill is reached, aim to the right of the farm buildings ahead. Pass through a metal gate and follow the waymarks to take the track ahead, which passes a tree-covered derelict building at Longshaw, and leads to another of the 'step-gates'. Pass through a gap in the fence to emerge at a road and turn left. Take the stile on the left opposite a gateway to a caravan park. Follow the hedge, keeping it on the right, to reach the road.

7. Cross over the road and go down the drive of Star Green Farm. Where the drive swings left, leave the drive and proceed ahead through a gate, over a stile and through a squeezer stile in quick succession to the field beyond. Follow the path down, with the wall on the right, pass through a section enclosed by walls on both sides, and continue with the hedge again on the right. Just before a copse, turn right over a step stile and a ladder stile and resume the original heading but with the wall now on the left. The path veers away from the wall to a stile under a holly tree, and passes to the right of the buildings ahead. Cross the driveway and go over a stile opposite to carry on down the right side of the hedge. Where the hedge bends round to the right, go through a gate on the left and head diagonally right, down to a ladder stile on to the road. The sign advertising the Lord Nelson Hotel is a good point to aim for.

8. Turn left to follow the road to Oakamoor. After passing the Cricketers' Arms, turn left immediately before the bridge at the Churnet Valley picnic site sign. Cross the field to a footbridge over the River Churnet and thus return to the car park.

Just before reaching the bridge, notice the stone pillars to the left. They are all that remains of the gates to the former copper works where the first transatlantic underwater communications cable was made.

Walk 6: Alton

Eugene Suggett and Jacquetta Fewster, Central Office

Starting point: Grid reference SK 074420, Alton Village Hall car park, at the corner of B5032 (Uttoxeter Road) and Hurstons Lane, Alton.

Distance: 6½ miles (10.5 kilometres)

Useful maps: Ordnance Survey Pathfinder 810 Ashbourne & the Churnet Valley, and Pathfinder 831 Uttoxeter, or Ordnance Survey Landranger 128 Derby and Burton upon Trent.

Terrain: Rolling pasture, ancient green lane, and some road walking.

---

1. Leave the car park and turn right to walk downhill along Lime Kiln Lane (the continuation of Uttoxeter Road). Follow the lane round to the right and continue up High Street. At the war memorial, turn right up the footpath, beside the cemetery, to Hurstons Lane. Cross over Hurstons Lane, slightly to the right, to a gate and stile.

2. Cross over the stile and bear slightly left to a metal gate at the jutting out corner of the field boundary.

   Note the fine views of the Weaver Hills on the left. The high rides of Alton Towers can also be seen; clanking and screaming from these may be heard.

   Go through the gate and walk towards the other end of the field, keeping the boundary on the left. Near the far corner, there is a stile on the left over which the Staffordshire Way passes. Do not go over the stile, but turn right to join the Staffordshire Way, which keeps close to the left-hand hedge for two fields, and cross the stile onto Saltersford Lane.

3. Turn left and walk along Saltersford Lane until the buildings of Holbrook Farm appear on the right.

Saltersford Lane is an old 'salt way' along which salt from Cheshire was conveyed by packhorse to Derbyshire and beyond.

Go through the double gates, leaving the Staffordshire Way, and follow the track between the buildings to the cattle grid. Continue on the track, which is the farm drive, to the road.

4. Cross the road to the stile directly opposite, and climb over it. Follow the path up the middle of the field to the top of the hill.

Turn to see another fine view of the Weaver Hills behind.

Pass through the gateway into the next field and, ignoring the cross path and keeping close to the hedge on the left, cross over two stiles. Denstone College comes into view.

Denstone College

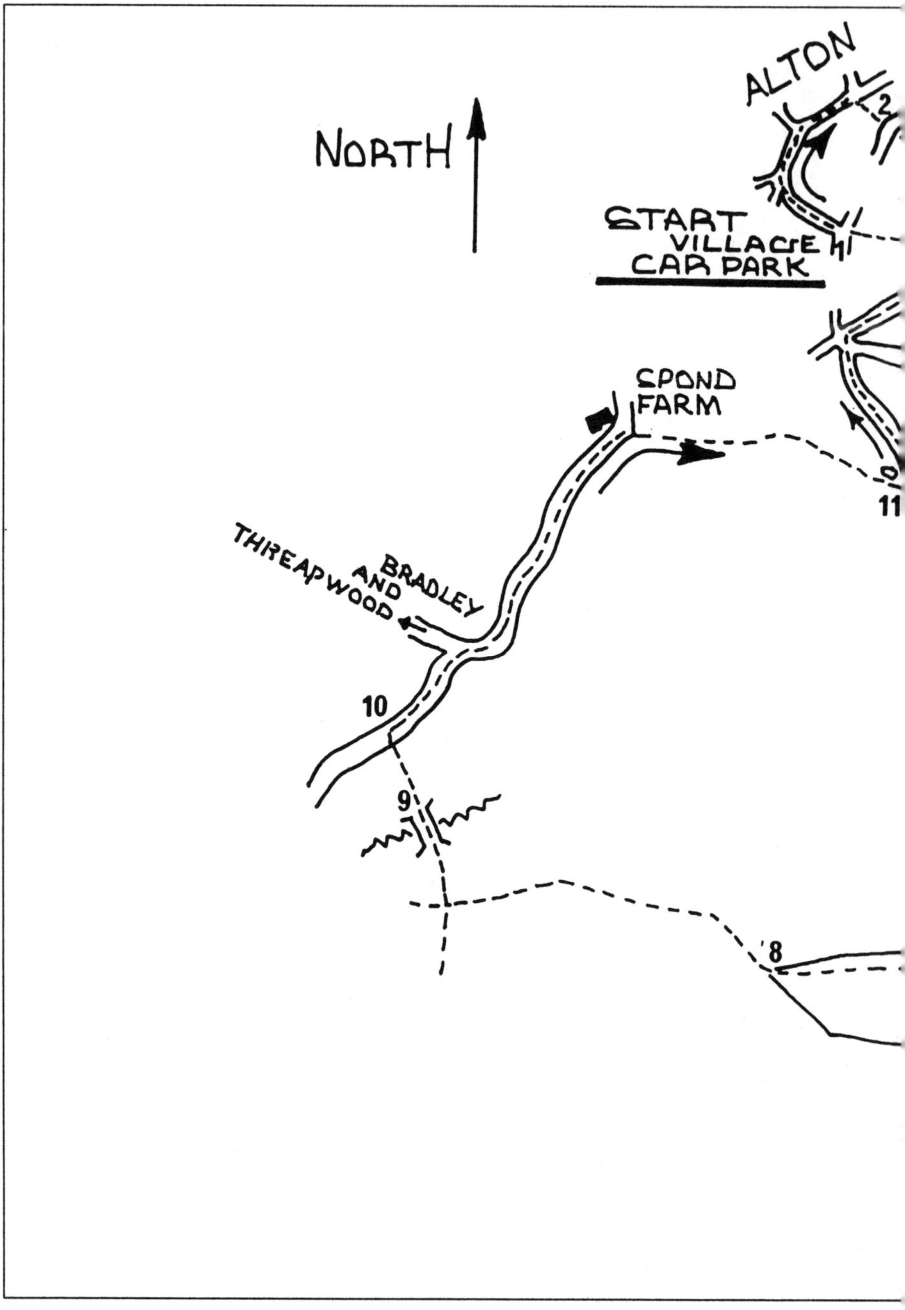
ALTON
NORTH
START
VILLAGE
CAR PARK
SPOND
FARM
BRADLEY
AND
THREAPWOOD
1
2
8
9
10
11

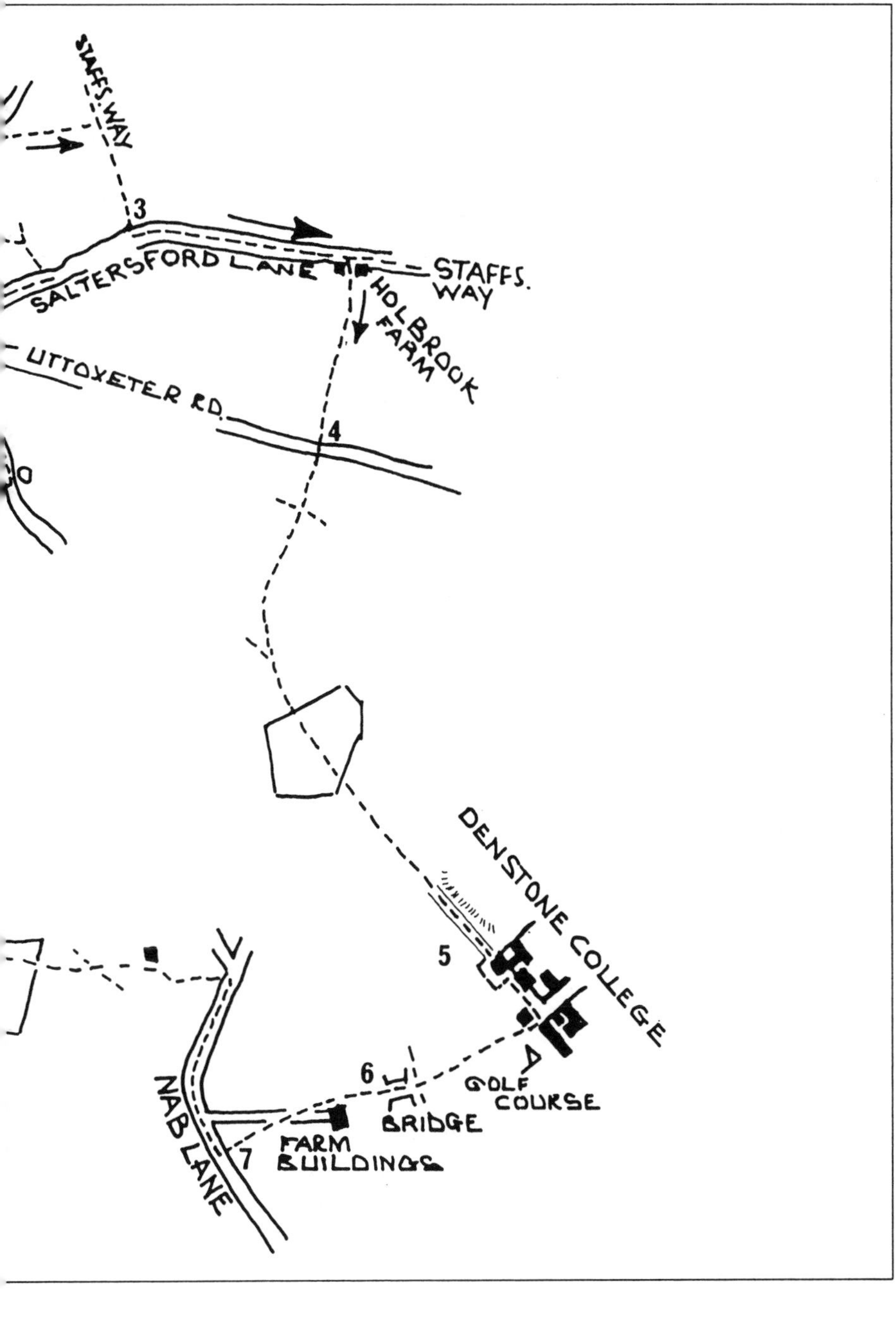
STAFFS WAY
3
SALTERSFORD LANE
STAFFS. WAY
HOLBROOK FARM
UTTOXETER RD.
4
DENSTONE COLLEGE
5
6
GOLF COURSE
BRIDGE
FARM BUILDINGS
7
NAB LANE

The Gothic-styled main building of the college dates from the early 1870's

Walk through the middle of this field, heading towards the left corner of the college building, to a stile in the far hedge. Cross over the stile, and keeping close to the left boundary of the field, cross over the stile into the next field. Keeping close to the hedge on the right, proceed to a gateway in the top right hand corner of the field.

5. Go through this into a short lane. Pass between the stone gate post on the left and the red brick wall on the right. Come down into a wide field, keeping close to the hedge on the left, and continue to a stile. Turn right and after a few metres turn left and walk beside the fence on the left with the golf course on the right. Continuing with the golf course on the right, keep close to the hedge, fence and embanked retaining wall on the left in front of the college.

Above, to the left, is a very moving warmemorial statue of a youthful St George. The statue is the work of sculptor Alfred Drury.

The path continues for a short distance through a garden to the left of a detached modern-looking bungalow. Leaving the garden, and just as a long white building looms up on the left, turn sharp right and head down through the golf course, towards an avenue of young trees. Walk through this avenue, and after that, close to an enclosure of conifers to the left. Coming close to the spinney at the bottom, the route crosses over the beginning of a red path, and then over a concrete bridge to a gate and a stile.

6. Cross the stile. Walk up the grassy lane and into an open field. Head across the field to a large tree, behind which is a gate and stile. Cross the stile and walk up beside the paddock on the left. Continue in this direction, crossing over the farm road, and coming beside a line of trees on the right. Walk beside these, keeping them on the right and cross the stile into Nabb Lane, a road.

7. Turn right onto the lane. The lane bends to the left and shortly afterwards to the right, then it goes gently downhill and bends left again. Here there is a skeletal Dutch barn on the right and a metal gate on the left. Go through the gate. Follow the track on the left side of the field. Just past some farm buildings on the right of the track, go through a gate or climb over its accompanying stile. Walk through the field, keeping close to the hedge on the left, to a metal bridle gate. Go through the gate, or over the stile beside it, and go straight ahead across the next field.

8. The path gradually gets closer to the hedge on the right-hand side until a small yellow gate down a bank in the far right corner of the field is reached. Go through this gate. The route continues onwards, on the crest of the hill, close to the left-hand hedge. Pass through three more gates. At the fourth, don't go through it, but turn sharp right down the hill to a beautiful stone squeeze stile in the bottom left corner of the field.

9. Walk down towards the woodlands across the narrow neck of the field, and cross the stream by the bridge. Follow close to the ditch on the lefthand side of the field. At the hedge at the top of the hill, turn right for a few steps, until another ancient stone squeeze stile is reached. Go through this onto the road.

10. Turn right and walk along the road ignoring the turn-off to Bradley and Threapwood. Follow the road to Spond Farm on the left. Just past the farm entrance, there is a gate on the right side of the road. Go through the gate. Follow the track ahead, to reach the end of a hedge standing marooned in the field, and keep this to the right. At the end of the field, enter the next field through the stone squeeze stile. Following the hedge on the left, pass through one stone stile and over two wooden ones. Continue by the hedge until an electricity pole is reached. Cross over the stile in the hedge at this point. The path continues diagonally to the right across this field, to the corner at the highest point of the field. Go through the stile onto the road.

11. Turn left down the road. At the crossroads, cross to Saltersford Lane, taking care on this awkward crossing. Walk down Saltersford Lane. Soon, the tarmac residential road turns into a peaceful track between the fields, much as the monks of Croxden would have known it. After a few minutes on the track, come to a stone squeeze stile on the left. Go through this. Do not go through the adjacent stone squeeze stile on the right, but walk up the hedgeline, keeping it on the right, to a wooden stile in the corner at the top. Cross this stile and turn left. Walk through the middle of the field to emerge from the field opposite the village hall at the end of Hurstons Lane.

Walk 7: Abbots Bromley

Ron Sayers, East Staffordshire Group

Starting point: Grid reference SK 080245, Butter Cross, Bagot Street, Abbots Bromley

Distance: 7 miles (11 kilometres)

Useful maps: Ordnance Survey Explorer 6 Cannock Chase and Chasewater, or Ordnance Survey Pathfinder 851 Abbots Bromley, or Ordnance Survey Landranger 128 Derby and Burton upon Trent

Terrain: Gently undulating with fine views of the countryside and reservoir. A stretch of the busy B5013 is used to cross the reservoir.

The Butter Cross, which dates back to the time of King Edward III, stands in the middle of what was once a busy market town with a weekly market. It is said that Dr Samuel Johnson, in his youth, helped his father to sell books under the Butter Cross. The nearby Goats Head Inn used to have a room named after Dick Turpin. The infamous highwayman is reputed to have stayed one night at the inn after stealing "Black Bess" from Rugeley Horse Fair.

1. From the Butter Cross, walk down the slope in front of the Goats Head public house, turn right at R & D Motors and go through the lych-gate into the churchyard.

Abbots Bromley parish church, dedicated to St Nicholas, took its shape mainly from its thirteenth century foundations. Over the years the church has been rebuilt, altered and repaired, and in 1850, under the guidance of George Street, there was a massive programme of restoration. It is worth stepping inside to appreciate the beauty of this church and to see the reindeer horns used in the famous Abbots Bromley Horn Dance, the

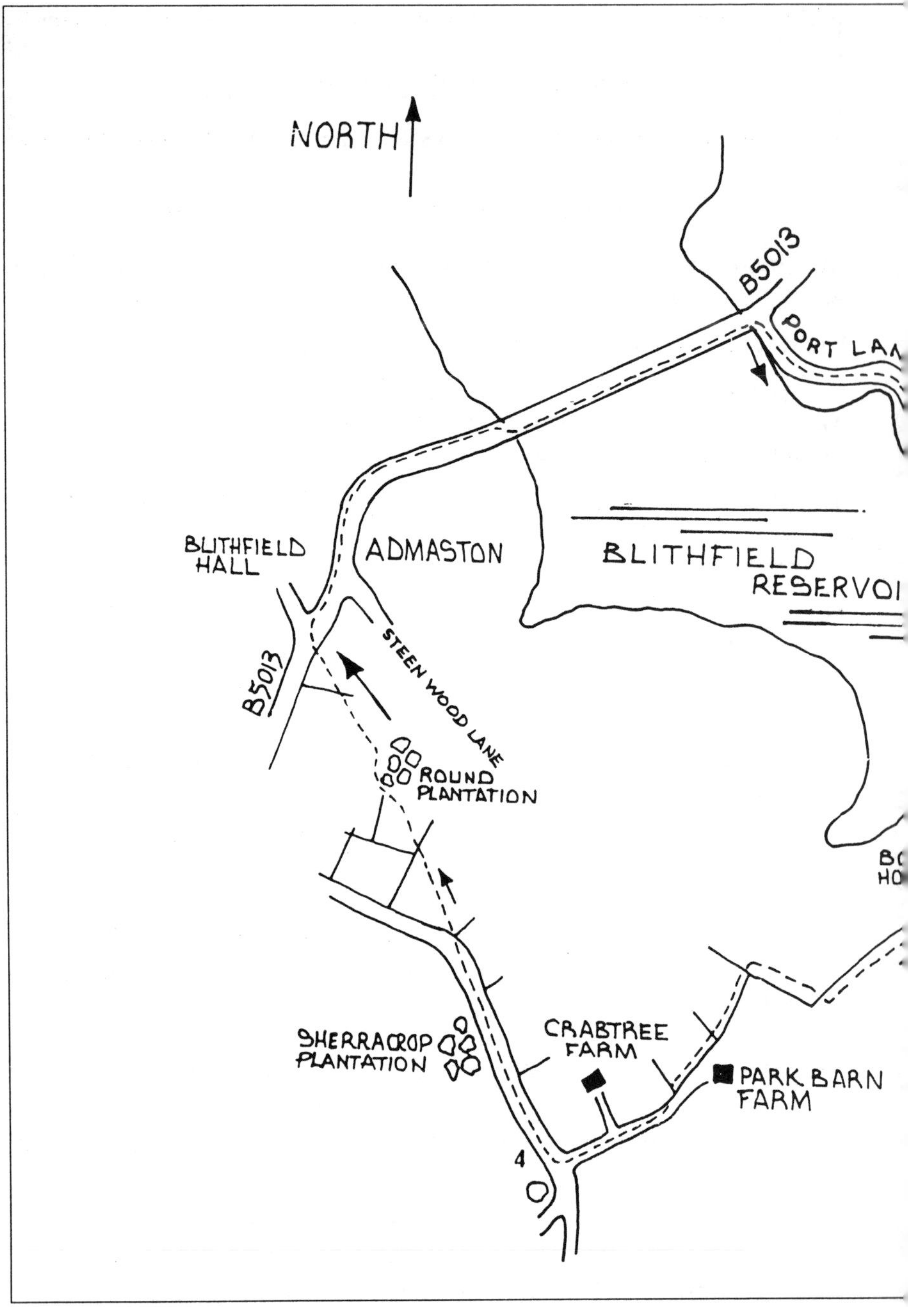
NORTH
B5013
PORT LAN
BLITHFIELD HALL
ADMASTON
BLITHFIELD
RESERVOI
B5013
STEEN WOOD LANE
ROUND PLANTATION
BO
HO
SHERRACROP PLANTATION
CRABTREE FARM
PARK BARN FARM
4

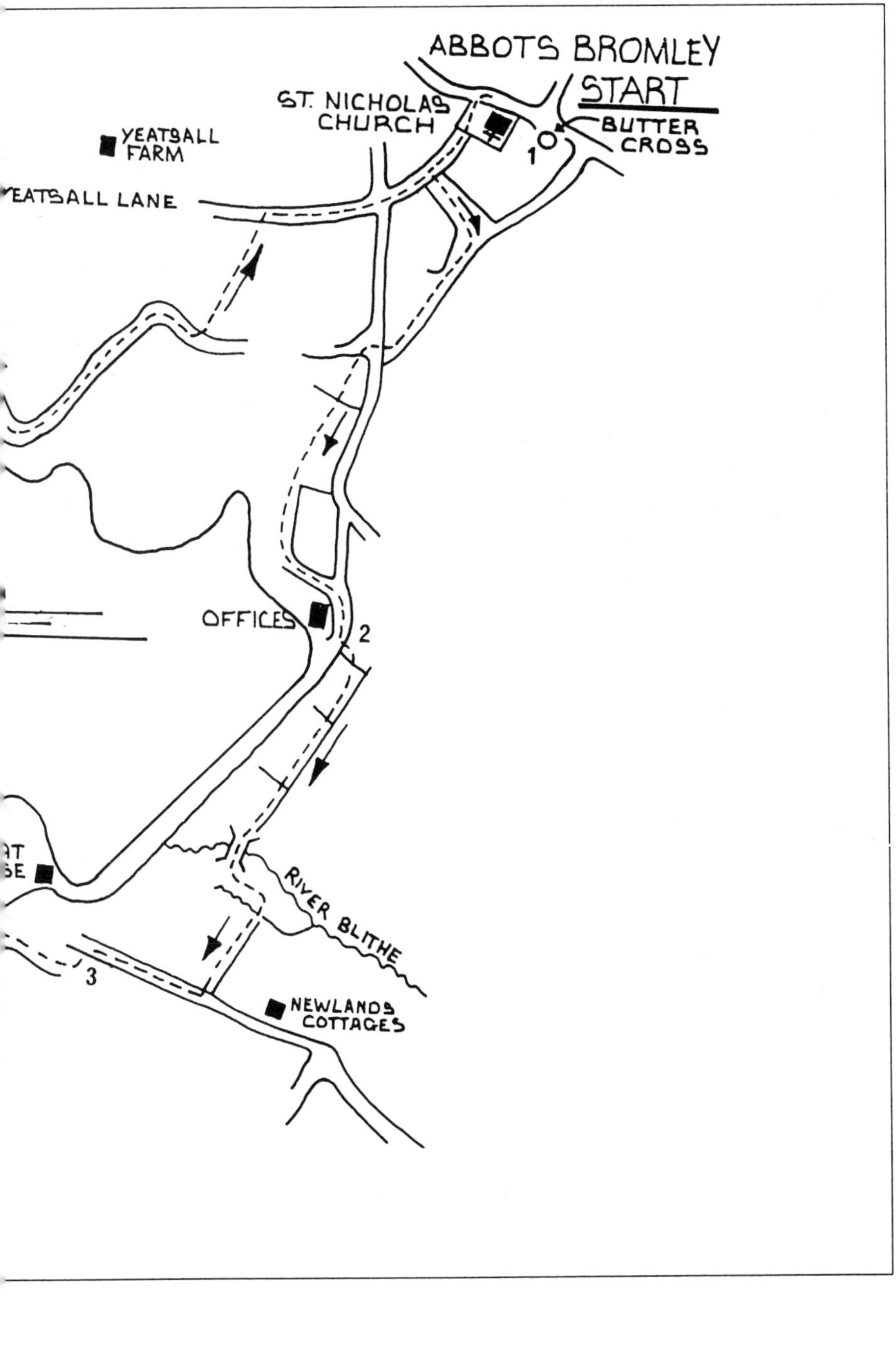
ABBOTS BROMLEY
START
ST. NICHOLAS CHURCH
BUTTER CROSS
1
YEATSALL FARM
EATSALL LANE
OFFICES
2
RIVER BLITHE
3
NEWLANDS COTTAGES

thirteenth century parish chest, and numerous other items of interest.

Follow the path to the right of the church, round the end of the church and down the slope to join the Staffordshire Way at the kissing gate at the far side of the churchyard. Continue along the path for 50 metres and climb the stile on the left. The path goes straight ahead across the field, midway between the stream and the hedge. Cross the bridge over the stream at the far end of the field, climb the stile, and turn right along the lane. When the concrete track bends right do not cross the cattle grid but go straight on, following the left hand fence to the road. Turn right and, after 80 metres, climb the stile on the left. Go straight ahead across two fields and over the stile at the bottom of the second field. Follow the hedge on your left which leads into a grassy lane with a stile at the end of it. Climb the stile and turn left along the lane and then turn right, along the road, towards Blithfield Reservoir Office.

2. Where the hedge on the left ends, turn left along the track for a few metres and then turn right to the stile in the hedge opposite. After the stile join the shale track which leads eventually to the concrete bridge over the River Blithe. Cross over the bridge, turn left along the river bank and, after 200 metres, as the river loops left, bear right across a plank bridge to a stile in the corner of the field. Go over the stile and follow the hedge on the left to the field corner then turn right along the track. After 400 metres, climb the stile on the left then turn right along the fence.

3. As the fence bears right, go straight ahead to the fence line on the bank, turn left, and follow the fence on the right up the hill.

As you look back, you enjoy fine views of Bagots Wood, the Blithe valley, and Blithfield reservoir which was created in 1953 when the river was dammed. The reservoir is popular for fishing, sailing, and bird watching, or as a spot for a simple picnic in peaceful surroundings. You will notice the trout hatcheries below the dam and herons are often to be seen sunning themselves on the bank or eagerly searching for fish.

Climb the stile by Medleywood Barn and continue along the fence on the right to the next field corner. Go over the stile and follow the hedge for 200 metres to a footbridge on the left. Once over the bridge, follow the ditch on the left through two fields to a stile leading into a lane. Go straight ahead along the lane to the road junction at Stockwell Heath.

4. At this T-junction turn right, leaving the Staffordshire Way, and walk along the Lane. Ignore the first stile on the right and carry on, over the hill, passing the Plantation on the left, to a stile on the right. Cross the field to a stile on the right of an old oak tree then cross to a stile at the left of Round Plantation. Continue in the same direction towards two Scots Pine trees on the horizon which are at the end of the drive to Blithfield Hall and climb over two stiles on the way.

Blithfield Hall has been the home of the Bagot family since 1360 and the grounds were home to the Bagot goats which, it is said, were originally given to Sir John Bagot by King Richard II in appreciation of the hunting he had enjoyed in Bagots Park. In recent years, the hall and other buildings have been converted into large flats and houses and the goats can only be seen at farms specialising in rare breeds.

On reaching the Rugeley-Uttoxeter Road (B5013) turn right and follow the roadside verges to the pavement over the reservoir. At the far end of the causeway turn right along the concrete road, which is Port Lane, and follow it for about mile (1¼ kilometres). After a bend to the right go over the stile on the left just at the top of the hill. Go straight across the field to a stile in the right hand corner leading into Yeatsall Lane. Turn right and, at the road junction, take the narrow tarmac path, almost opposite, into the churchyard and back to the Butter Cross.

If time permits it is worth walking along Bagot Street to see the almshouses which were a gift to the village by Lambert Bagot in 1705 and also the beautiful timbered building, Church House, which was built in 1619. In the opposite direction, past the village green and war memorial, is High Street where there are also buildings of architectural interest. The school of St Mary and St Anne is on both sides of the road. St Anne's was opened in 1874 and St Mary's in 1882 and the two were amalgamated in 1921 to form the present girls' school.

Walk 8: Colton

Bill Simmons, Lichfield Group

Starting point: Grid reference SK 049213, lay-by for the Staffordshire Way, Stockwell Heath Lane. Travelling from Abbots Bromley along the B5013, take the third road on the left after crossing the reservoir. The lay-by is on the right.

Distance: 7.5 miles (12 kilometres)

Useful maps: Ordnance Survey Explorer 6 Cannock Chase and Chasewater, or Ordnance Survey Pathfinder 851 Abbots Bromley, or Ordnance Survey Landranger 128 Derby and Burton upon Trent

Terrain: Open, undulating countryside and quiet country lanes.

---

1. Leave the lay-by and turn right. Go along the lane to re-join the Staffordshire Way briefly at Stockwell Heath. At the T-junction by the pond, turn left. After the first corner bear left, leaving the Staffordshire Way, and walk half-way up the hill then go over the stile on the right. Keep to the hedge on the right and go over two more stiles then pass a tree-covered area on higher ground and go over the stile at the highest point. Go straight across the next field to another stile to the left of the cottages.

2. At the lane turn left. After about three-quarters of a mile (1.25 kilometres) the lane ends at a road junction in Admaston. Cross the busy road carefully to reach the telephone box then go down the lane, School Lane, slightly to the left and follow it to the end.

   In the Spring the snowdrops along this lane are a delight to see.

   The path is to the left of the old school. From the bridle gate, cross the field to the sign, go over the tarmac drive and turn

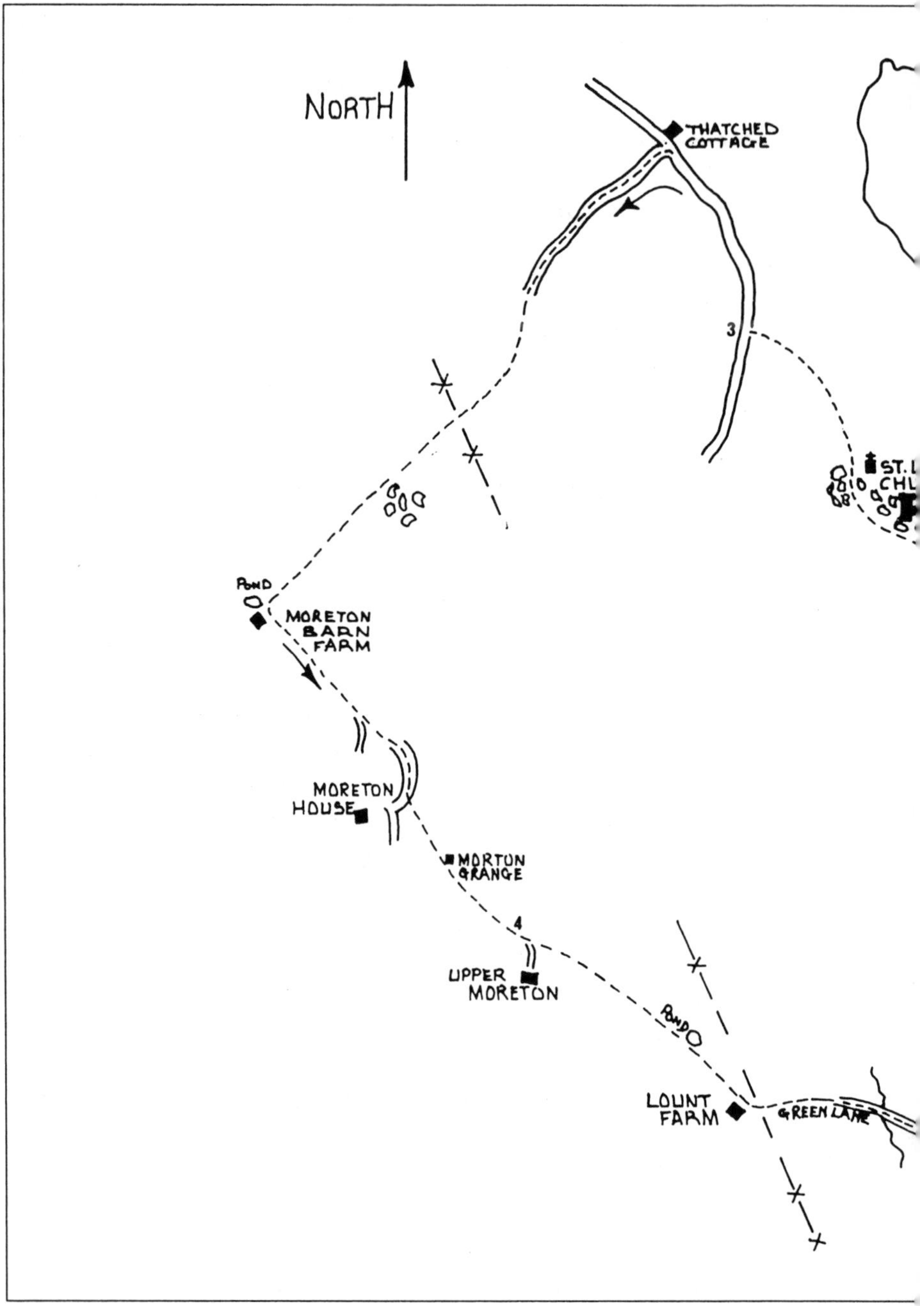
NORTH
THATCHED COTTAGE
3
POND
MORETON BARN FARM
MORETON HOUSE
MORTON GRANGE
4
UPPER MORETON
POND
LOUNT FARM
GREEN LANE

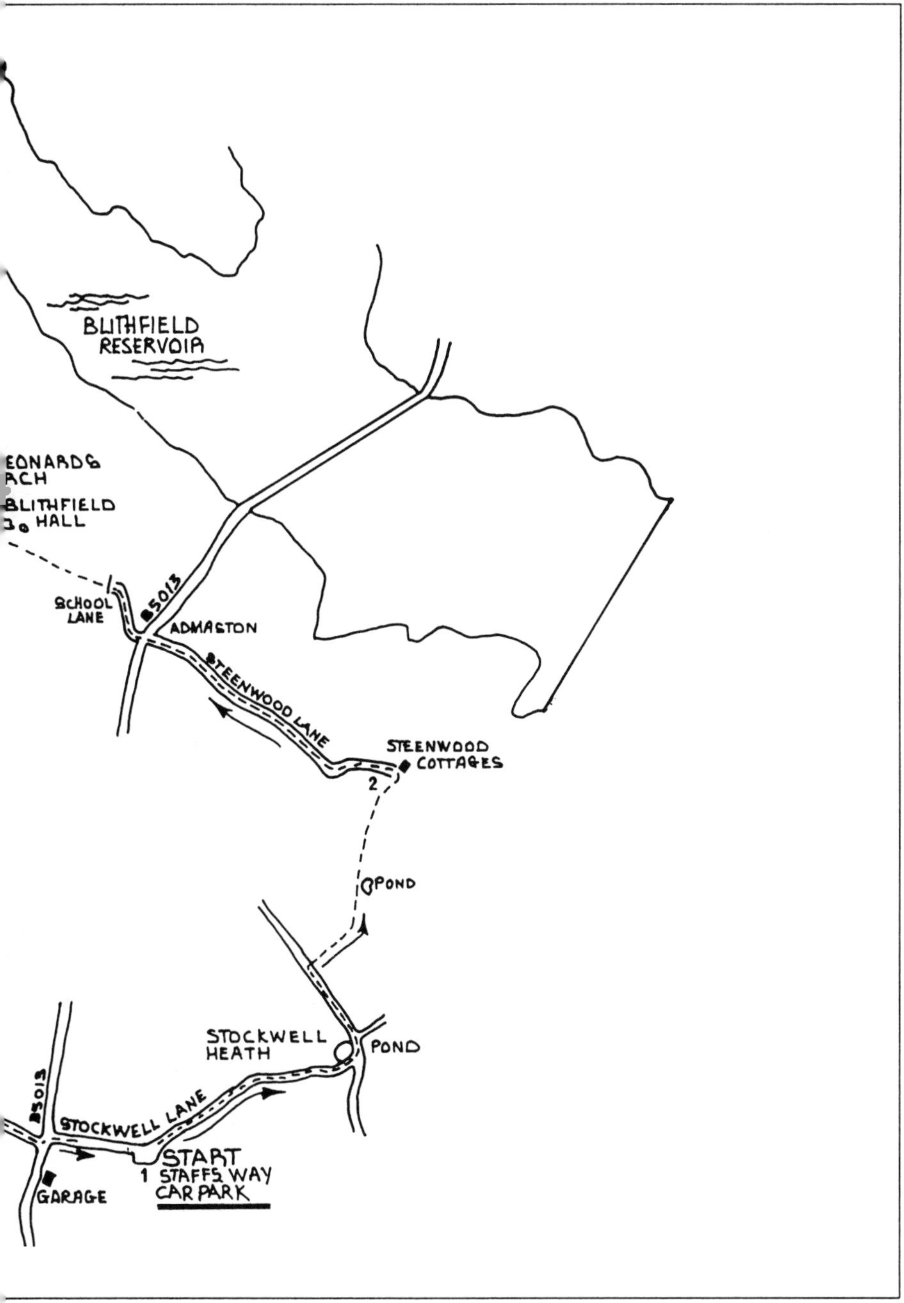
BLITHFIELD RESERVOIR
EONARDS
ACH
BLITHFIELD
HALL
SCHOOL LANE
B5013
ADMASTON
STEENWOOD LANE
STEENWOOD COTTAGES
2
POND
STOCKWELL HEATH
POND
B5013
STOCKWELL LANE
START
1 STAFFS WAY CAR PARK
GARAGE

half right to cross diagonally to the opposite hedge. Pass through the bridle gate in the hollow. Cross the field to reach a gate and stile just to the left of the tree-line ahead. Go over the stile and follow the ha-ha and wall.

Notice the burnt bricks from the coal-fired kilns at the time that the Hall was first built.

Go through the gate to come to St Leonard's Church.

To the left is the old Rectory, now converted into flats and, to the right, beyond the church is Blithfield Hall and Blithfield reservoir.

Cross the cattle grid ahead and follow the lane to the road.

3. Turn right and walk as far as the thatched cottage on the right. Turn left and go down the bridle path. Go through the gate at the end of the track and follow the hedge on the right. There are two stiles to cross before passing over the footbridge in the bottom corner. At first, keep to the hedge on the left then take the track up to the farm at the top of the hill. Turn left just before the hay barn and keep to the hedge on the left. Pass through the gates and walk up the track towards another farm at a high point. Where the track swings right to climb up to the farm, leave the track and continue ahead to a stile in the corner of the field. Go over the stile, and follow the boundary on the left to a gate at the side of a cottage. Go through the gate and onto a track. Turn right and follow the track to the cattle grid and its accompanying bridle gate. Turn left and after the next bridle gate go to the farm gate at the bottom of the hill. Pass through the barn yard. Ahead is a farm track passing some houses and leading to Upper Moreton Farm.

4. Follow the track keeping to the hedge on the left until there is a bend with a stile and field gate on the left. Go over the stile and keep to the left hedge as far as the bottom corner. In the next field follow the hedge to the right and then go through the gate into a green lane. At a junction of tracks by a farm on the right, turn left and join a tarmac track across the meadows leading to the Rugeley – Abbots Bromley road.

5. Turn left then cross the road carefully. Go down Stockwell Lane to return to the lay-by for the Staffordshire Way.

Walk 9: Trent and Mersey Canal

Bill Simmons, Lichfield Group

Starting point: Grid reference SK 049213, lay-by for the Staffordshire Way, Stockwell Heath Lane. Travelling from Abbots Bromley along the B5013, take the third road on the left after crossing the reservoir. The lay-by is on the right.

Distance: 8 miles (13 kilometres)

Useful maps: Ordnance Survey Explorer 6, Cannock Chase and Chasewater, or Ordnance Survey Pathfinder 851 Abbots Bromley, or Ordnance Survey Landranger 128 Derby and Burton upon Trent

Terrain: Open, undulating countryside including sections at the side of the Trent and Mersey canal and the river Trent.

---

1. Leave the lay-by and turn left. Walk along Stockwell Heath Lane to the T-junction with the Abbots Bromley – Rugeley Road. Cross the road carefully, turn left then immediately right down the lane and along a field track. Continue to some farm buildings. Turn right in front of the buildings and continue along a green lane to the end. Go through the gate on the right and follow the hedge to the left heading for the gate in the far right corner. Go through the gate, turn left and follow the hedge on the left boundary. Pass through two gates to reach a green track and continue ahead to a pond in the field. Turn right, keep to the hedge on the left boundary for two fields until the hedge line by the pylon is reached.

The skyline ahead gives splendid views of Cannock Chase.

Go through the gate in the left corner of the field, pass a pool and go along a tree-lined green track on the left to reach a bridle gate. Turn right along a fenced track passing through two more bridle gates to reach the road.

2. Go along the road with the main railway line on the left and turn left at the T-junction then cross over the railway bridge. Go over a stile on the right after the first length of hedgerow. Follow the hedge on the right of the field. Climb one stile, and keep the fence on the right. In the corner of the field cross the stile into the field next to the railway. Follow the fence on the left up to the gate, go straight across the field then pass over two stiles next to the buildings ahead. Continue in the same direction to follow the rough road to the main A51 road. Turn left and walk at the roadside for a few metres to reach a point opposite a road junction. Taking great care, cross the busy main road and walk along the pavement of the minor road to the school.

3. Cross the road to the church, turn right then left after the parking area and follow the path to the stile. Go across the field and over the Trent and Mersey canal bridge. Turn left along the tow path which is part of the Staffordshire Way.

4. Continue along the canal with the river Trent on the right, passing under bridges number 70 and 69, to reach bridge number 68 a "turn-over bridge" near Colton.

A "turn over bridge" is where a horse pulling a narrow boat, could cross from one side of the canal to the towpath on the other side without tangling the tow rope on the bridge. The horse would pass under the bridge then turn right to go over the bridge. Notice the grooves in the brick work due to the wear of the towing rope as the horse turned right to continue pulling the boat on the other side of the canal.

After passing over the canal bridge, continue along the lane, over the railway bridge to the road.

5. Turn left, walk on the tarmac footpath and go past the entrance to Rugeley Lodge. Continue along the tarmac footpath,

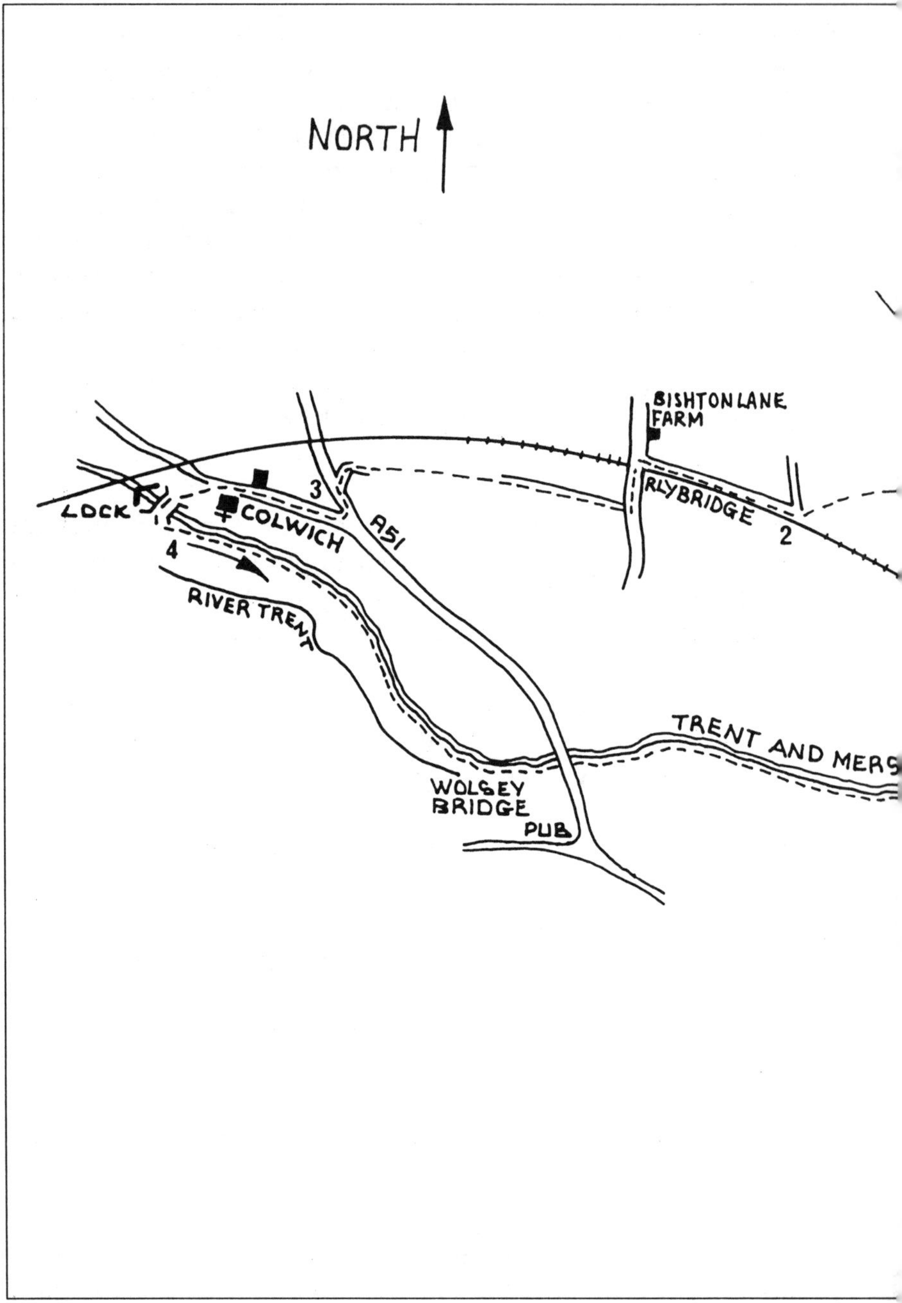
NORTH
BISHTON LANE FARM
LOCK
3
COLWICH
A51
RLY BRIDGE
2
4
RIVER TRENT
TRENT AND MERS
WOLSEY BRIDGE
PUB

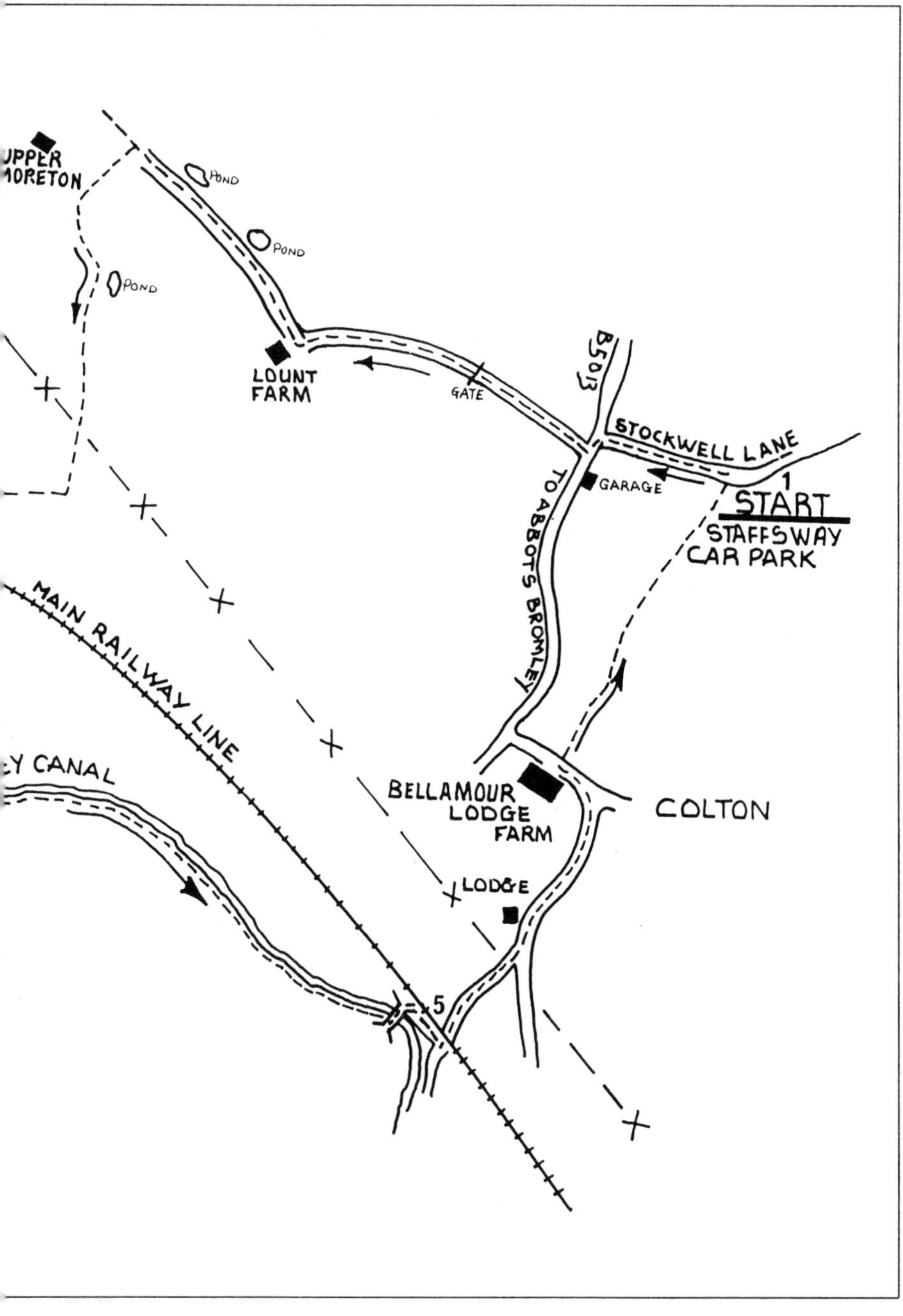
UPPER
MORETON
POND
POND
POND
LOUNT
FARM
GATE
B5013
STOCKWELL LANE
GARAGE
1
START
STAFFSWAY
CAR PARK
TO ABBOTS BROMLEY
MAIN RAILWAY LINE
EY CANAL
BELLAMOUR
LODGE
FARM
COLTON
LODGE
5

passing a minor road junction on the right, and go round a left hand bend.

The Staffordshire Way, as it is now defined, turns off to the right along the minor road. The route described here follows the Staffordshire Way as it was originally defined. Evidence of the earlier route can still be detected on some of the signposts and waymarks.

The tarmac path finishes just round the bend but continue on the grassy wayside to a farm on the left. Cross the road carefully to the stile. Go over the stile and continue just past the end of the hedge on the right to where there is a stile. Go over the stile, turn left and keep by the fence on the left to another stile ahead. Go over the stile, cross the concrete bridge and go through the gate on the other side. Keeping the boundary and the stream on the left, continue over a stile to a kissing gate in the field corner. Go through the kissing gate, cross the plank bridge and go over the stile on the other side. Follow the hedge on the left to a kissing gate beside a field gate. Go through the kissing gate to return to the start of the walk.

Walk 10: Shugborough Park

Geoff and Margaret Loadwick,
Stoke/Newcastle Group

Starting point: Grid Reference SJ 973210, Milford Common car park. Milford is four miles (six kilometres) from Stafford and lies on the A513 Stafford to Rugeley road. Travelling from Stafford, turn right at Milford Common into Brocton Road. The entrance to the car park is on the left.

Distance: 5 miles (10 kilometres)

Useful maps: Ordnance Survey Explorer 6 Cannock Chase and Chasewater, or Ordnance Survey Pathfinder 850 Stafford, or Ordnance Survey Landranger 127 Stafford, Telford & surrounding area.

Terrain: Mostly level walking on good paths but there is a long gentle climb and a short steep climb to viewpoints, towards the end of the walk.

---

1. Facing away from Stafford and with the rising ground of Cannock Chase on the right, walk diagonally left across the flat expanse of the common to reach the A513 road. Cross this busy road carefully to a grassy triangle. Walk across the grass to the apex of the triangle where two minor roads meet and there is a signpost. One arm points to Tixall and Great Haywood. Follow the pavement in this direction.

This is a narrow road. At first there is a pavement on the left but when this ends, it is probably safer to continue along the left verge of the road instead of following the normal procedure and walking on the right.

Soon the road crosses a railway and in a further 200 metres it crosses the River Sow. One hundred metres further still, there is a third bridge. Do not cross this bridge but go down the steps on the left leading to the towpath of the Staffordshire & Worcestershire canal.

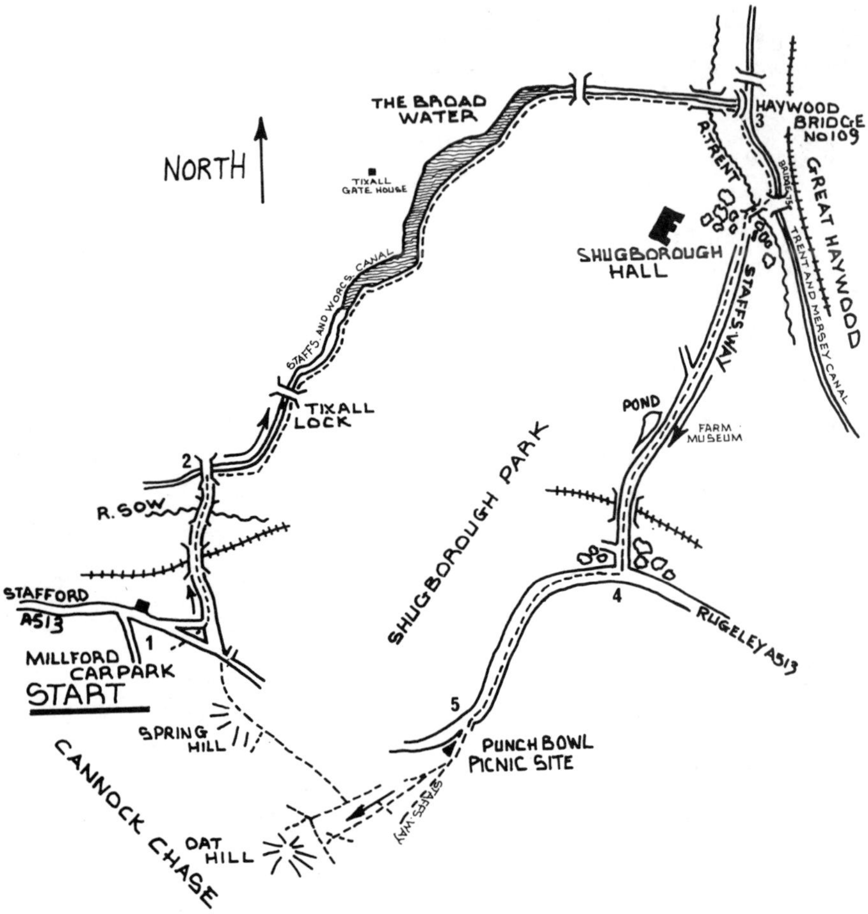

2. Walk under the bridge and follow the towpath. The towpath continues past Tixall Lock and Tixall Broad and crosses the River Trent before reaching the junction with the Trent & Mersey canal at Great Haywood.

Tixall Broad or 'The Broad Water' as it is shown on the Explorer map, forms a very picturesque length of the canal. It was designed to look like a lake, specially to satisfy the demands of the landowner who did not want the view from Tixall Hall spoiled by the canal. Sadly, little more than the stables and the gatehouse of the hall now remain. They can be seen across the fields on the other side of the canal.

3. At the junction, go under the bridge, Haywood Bridge, bridge number 109, and turn right to follow the tow path of the Trent & Mersey canal to the next lock at a stone bridge, bridge number 73. Pass under the bridge and immediately turn right onto the Staffordshire Way. On the right there is a gap in the wall by the side of a gate. Go through the gap onto the road and turn left. In a few metres pass over Essex Bridge and enter the grounds of Shugborough Park.

Essex bridge takes its name from the Earls of Essex who had it built in the 17th century. This packhorse bridge is believed to have had forty-three arches when it was constructed; now only fourteen remain, but it is still reputed to be the longest packhorse bridge in England. The confluence of the rivers Sow and Trent is just to the right of the bridge.

Shugborough Hall, now the property of the National Trust, has been associated with the Anson family, later to become 'Earls of Lichfield', since 1642. The Hall, which can be clearly seen from the drive, has been re-modeled several times. The columns of the portico are each single oaks covered in slate.

Continue along the drive. Ignore the road entering from the right that carries vehicles leaving Shugborough Hall car park. Pass Shugborough Park Farm which is on the right and the Farm car park which is on the left and then cross the bridge over the main Euston to Crewe railway track.

The tunnel that takes the railway through Shugborough Park owes its existence, not to any physical conditions of the

Shugborough Hall

terrain, but to the demands of the landowner who did not want the presence of the railway to spoil the view from the Hall. The east end of the tunnel is just visible from the drive.

Just after crossing the railway, the drive turns sharply to the right. Do not turn right, but leave the tarmac drive and continue straight ahead for 100 metres to the Stafford – Rugeley road.

4. Turn right and follow the pavement and when that ends continue along the grass verge at the side of the road. Near the brow of the hill, when it is safe to do so, cross the road carefully and follow the wide grass verge on the other side. Where the road bends sharply to the right, in a dip, leave the road and follow the track into the Punch Bowl car park and picnic site.

The Punch Bowl lies on the northern fringe of Cannock Chase which covers an area of approximately 26 square miles and at one time formed part of a much larger royal hunting forest where King Henry II hunted deer. Cannock Chase was designated as an Area of Outstanding Natural Beauty in 1958. Two-thousand five-hundred acres of the Chase forms the Cannock Chase Country Park which is owned and managed by Staffordshire County Council as public access land.

5. Follow the broad track up the hill and go past the wooden car barrier. At this point leave the Staffordshire Way by turning off the main track and ascending a grassy track sloping up through the birch trees to the right. Where the broad track splits four ways, take the path that slopes up to the right. Near the top of the hill, Oat Hill, a broad path comes in from the left; follow this path to the right for thirty metres to meet a cross path.

Ahead, across the path, there is a small enclosed conifer plantation. In clear weather it is rewarding to make a small detour by walking around the perimeter of the plantation to admire the distant views of the Shropshire Hills and the Welsh border to the west, and the Weaver Hills to the north. After the detour, return to the cross path and turn to face the plantation.

6. Turn right and walk down the broad stony path. Ignore the track off to the right after thirty metres. Continue downhill to a broad cross-track and turn right. At the first junction, where a path comes in from the right, turn left and continue downhill. At the next junction, keep left and continue down the hill. Descend some steps to a narrow saddle and climb the steps ahead to the top of Spring Hill.

This is a good view point from which can be seen the conical shape of the Wrekin and Stafford castle to the west, and below in the foreground, can be seen the canal, the river Sow and the railway line all in close proximity to each other.

To descend, face away from the steps and follow the broad path down the slope on the right to a conifer wood. Turn left in front of the wood and descend some wooden steps. At the bottom, turn right and follow the path at the edge of the wood. At the corner of the wood, just before a shallow grassy depression, the path divides. Follow the narrow path to the left for a few metres to arrive at the edge of Milford Common, near the starting point.

Walk 11: Acton Trussell and Bednall

David and Janet Palmer, Mid-Staffordshire Group

Starting point: Grid Reference SJ 937169, on the road between Penkridge and Brocton in the lay-by made from the former road either side of canal bridge number 91 at Shutt Hill Lock. (Shown as Shutthill on Ordnance Survey maps.)

Distance: 6.5 miles (10.5 kilometres)

Useful maps: Ordnance Survey Explorer 6 Cannock Chase and Chasewater, or Ordnance Survey Pathfinder 871 Cannock (North), or Ordnance Survey Landranger 127 Stafford, Telford & surrounding area.

Terrain: Mostly flat and including a canal towpath, park land, and cultivated fields.

1. Walk along the towpath of the Staffordshire & Worcestershire Canal towards Penkridge with the canal on the left.

   James Brindley, the father of canals in Britain, had an ambition to join the four great rivers, Mersey, Trent, Severn and Thames by inland waterways. The Staffordshire & Worcestershire Canal, whose construction was authorised in 1766, was part of this scheme. It links the Trent & Mersey Canal to the Severn at Stourport but it was not until 1790, seventeen years after Brindley's death that the scheme was completed with a link to the Thames at Oxford.

   Leave at the next bridge, number 90, Park Gate, and go over the bridge to join the Staffordshire Way. Go over a stile at the side of a metal gate and shortly afterwards go over another stile into a field. Follow the Staffordshire Way diagonally left to a footbridge in the far corner of the field on the skyline.

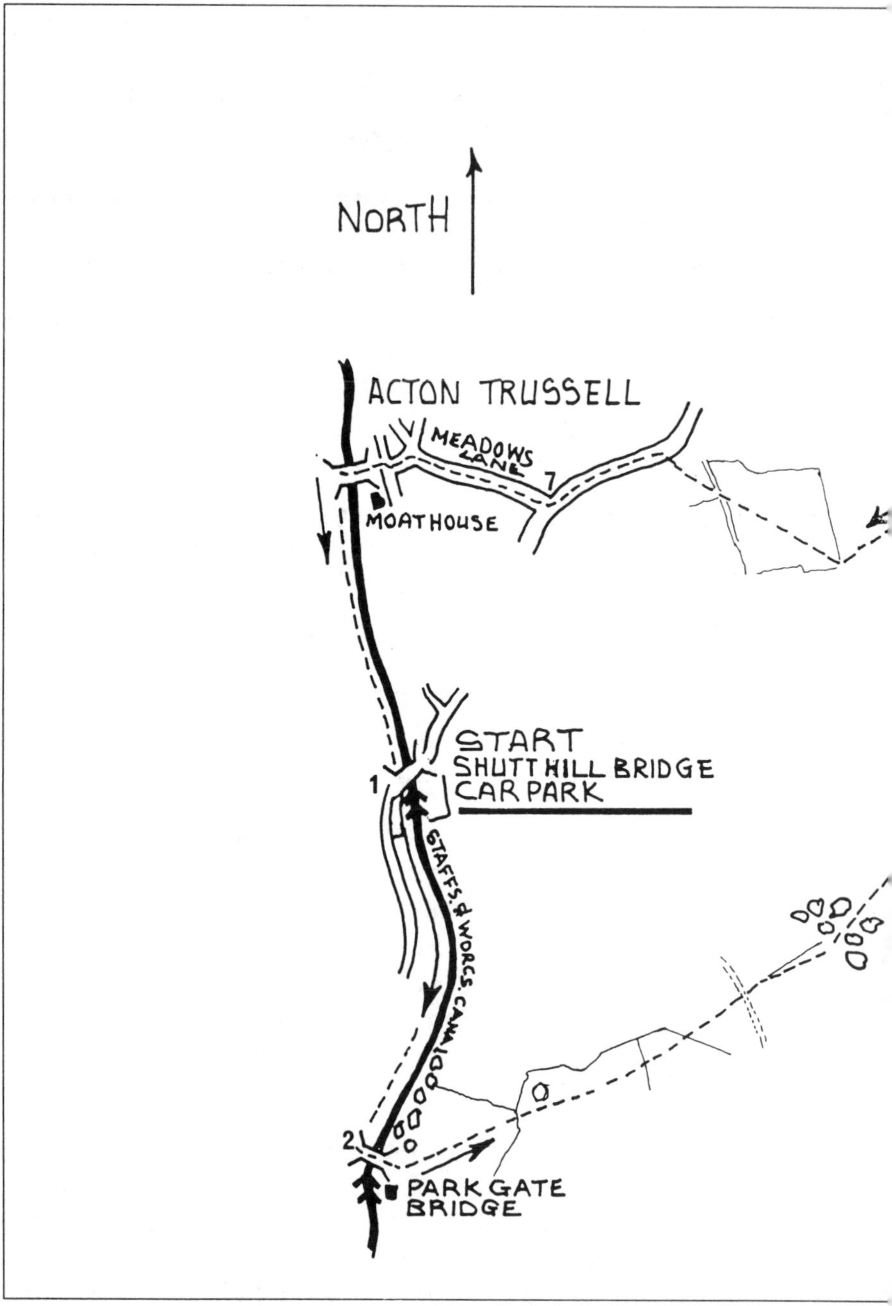
NORTH
ACTON TRUSSELL
MEADOWS LANE
7
MOATHOUSE
START
SHUTT HILL BRIDGE
CAR PARK
1
STAFFS. & WORCS. CANAL
2
PARK GATE
BRIDGE

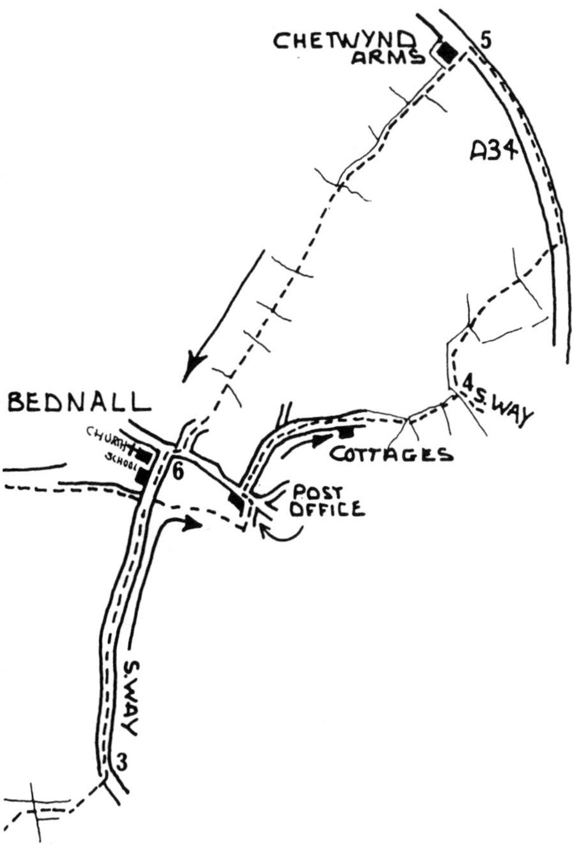
CHETWYND
ARMS
5
A34
BEDNALL
CHURCH
SCHOOL
6
4
S.WAY
COTTAGES
POST
OFFICE
S.WAY
3

(The farmer often asks walkers to go round the edge of the field)

2. Cross the footbridge and turn left following the Staffordshire Way sign along the edge of the field to a stile on the left. Cross the stile and walk beside the hedge on the right hand side of the field. When the hedge turns right, keep straight ahead to a stile. Cross the farm track and go over another stile into a field. Cross the field, with the fence on the right, and enter the wood by a stile. Walk through the wood to a stile. Cross the stile and keep in the same direction to a stile near an old sandstone gate post. Cross this stile and keeping the hedge on the right walk to a lane.

3. Turn left and follow the lane to Bednall. The church spire should be in sight after the first bend.

   Bednall is an attractive little village with a shop, primary school, and church. The church was built in 1846 although the steeple dates from 1873.

   At the edge of the village, where the verge on the right of the road ends, leave the Staffordshire Way and cross a stile beside a holly hedge on the right. Follow the left edge of the field behind the houses and turn left through a gate to a road beside the village Post Office and shop. Turn left along the road and immediately right to rejoin the Staffordshire Way along a track. Follow the track, forking right at a junction and passing some cottages on the right. The track ends with a stile leading into a field. Cross the stile and keep on the right side of the field to a stile in the corner. Do not cross the stile.

4. Turn left in front of the stile, leaving the Staffordshire Way, and follow the edge of the field round to a gate. Go through the gate and follow the hedge on the left for approximately fifty metres to the next gate. Here turn to the right and walk across the field to the hedge opposite. Turn left along the edge

of the field to a stile and footbridge on the right. Go over the bridge and cross the field to a stile just to the right of a prominent road sign on the main A34 road. Turn left along the footpath beside the road to the Chetwynd Arms public house.

5. Turn left immediately before the public house and walk down the side of the building to a stile. Cross this stile into a field and continue with the hedge on the right through two more fields to a double stile and footbridge over a stream. The footpath leads up the slope and passes just to the left of a prominent tree on the skyline. Continue past the tree to a stile beside a round water trough. Cross over this stile and continue in the same direction crossing two more stiles to reach a footbridge. Keep forward towards Bednall and cross one more stile before arriving at some farm buildings. Turn right over a stile in the hedge in front of the farm buildings. Keep left by the hedge to a stile beside a bungalow. Cross the stile and follow the path down to a gate into Bednall village.

6. Cross the road and follow the footpath round to the left. Go past the school and turn down the first track on the right just before the house named "Fieldfare". The footpath follows this track which soon turns to the left and ends at a field gate. At the gate, the path changes direction again and turns right. Do not go through the gate but go over the stile at the side of the gate and follow the hedge, keeping it on the left. Cross several stiles before arriving at a stile with a bridge over a stream. Cross the field diagonally right to the right hand side of a line of poplars where there is a stile leading to a farm track. The footpath ends on the right where the farm track meets the road.

7. Turn left and follow the road to the first turning on the right, Meadow Lane. Follow the lane to Acton Trussell.

This delightful village has a long history stretching back at least to the Iron Age as is evidenced by the discovery of Iron age pottery and flints. The remains of a second century Roman villa were found under the church. The church itself, which has a 16th century tower, was restored by George Edmund Street who built the Law Courts in London. The moated manor house, now the Moat House restaurant, has recently been refurbished and its timber frame is believed to have been constructed in the early 14th century. The first record of the Trussells at Acton is in 1342 when John Trussell settled the Manor of Acton (with Bednall and Brocton) on himself and his wife.

In the village, turn left at the telephone box and at the T-junction turn right into Lower Penkridge Road and then immediately left down a footpath. At canal bridge 92, Acton Moat, turn right onto the towpath and go under the bridge. Walk to the next bridge at Shutt Hill Lock where the walk started.

Walk 12: Wheaton Aston

Rob and Celia Cox, Mid-Staffordshire Group

Starting point: Grid Reference SJ 853126, Village Hall car park, Hawthorn Road, Wheaton Aston

Distance: 9 miles (14.5 kilometres)

Useful maps: Ordnance Survey Pathfinder 871 Cannock (North), or Ordnance Survey Landranger 127 Stafford, Telford & surrounding area

Terrain: Mostly flat with some towpath walking.

Note: Since this description was written, Staffordshire County Council has placed a six-month temporary closure order on the bridleway from Shredicote Hall Farm because the bridge over Church Eaton brook has become unsafe. Before undertaking the walk it would be wise to check with Christine Cheeseman at Staffordshire County Council, tel: 01785 277247, to determine whether the bridleway has been reopened.

1. Turn left from the car park and walk to the village square. Take the first road on the left, School Road, and follow it as it becomes a green lane. Continue for half a mile ($^3/_4$ kilometre), ignoring the footpath on the left, to a bridle gate on a bend. Go through the gate and cross the field to a bridle gate in the far hedge. Go through the gate to arrive at a crossing point of bridleways. Turn left and walk along the avenue of trees.

   This is the Monks Walk which was used in medieval times for monks to walk from Lapley, where there was a Benedictine priory, to Blackladies.

2. Keeping the hedge on the left, continue to a bridle gate. Follow the concrete road to the left for approximately 50 metres, then

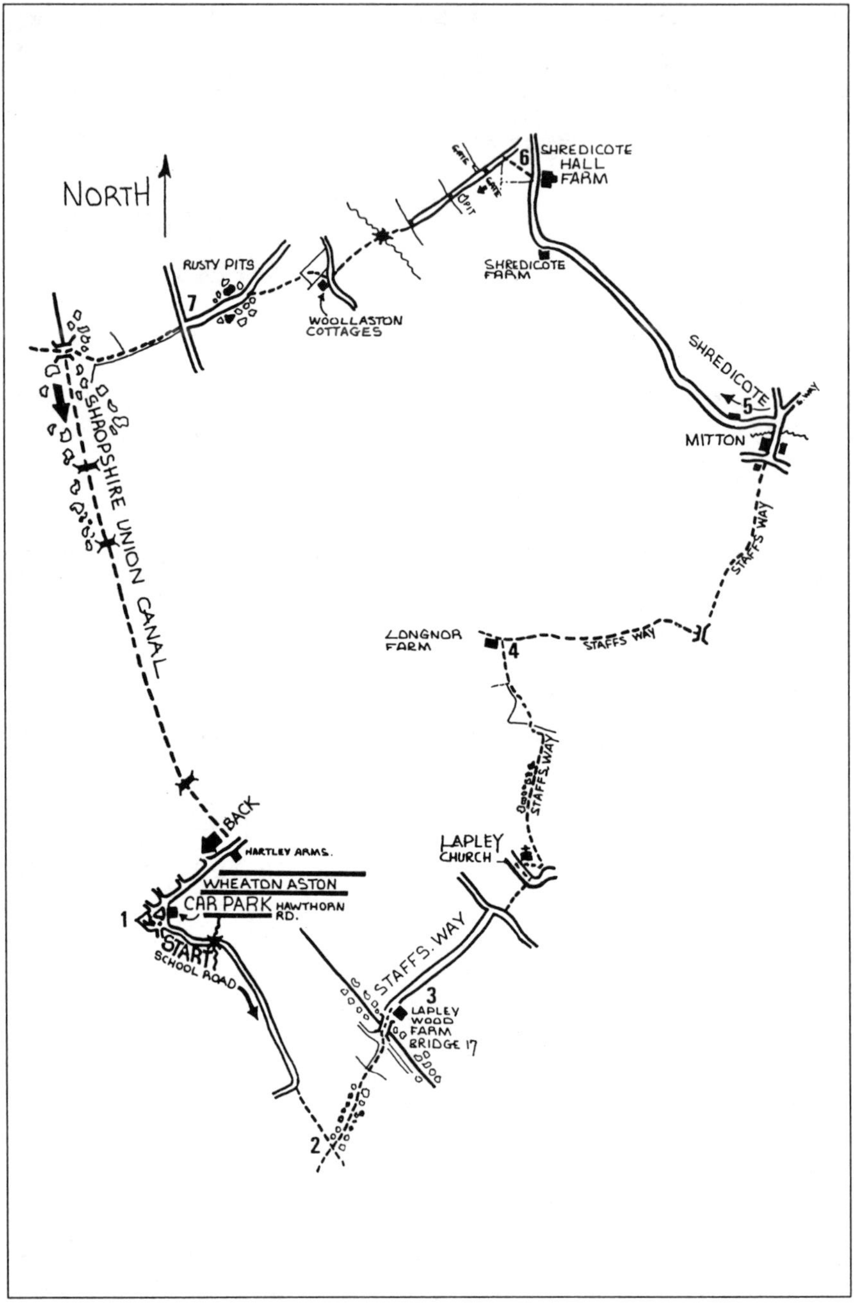
NORTH
SHREDICOTE HALL FARM
SHREDICOTE FARM
6
RUSTY PITS
7
WOOLLASTON COTTAGES
SHREDICOTE
5
MITTON
SHROPSHIRE UNION CANAL
STAFFS WAY
LONGNOR FARM
4
STAFFS WAY
STAFFS WAY
BACK
HARTLEY ARMS.
LAPLEY CHURCH
WHEATON ASTON
CAR PARK
HAWTHORN RD.
1
START
SCHOOL ROAD
STAFFS. WAY
3
LAPLEY WOOD FARM
BRIDGE 17
2

turn right through the gate in the trees and go over the canal bridge. Carry straight on to Lapley Wood Farm to join the Staffordshire Way.

3. Pass through the farmyard and walk along the farm drive to the road. Cross the road and turn right.

This road follows the line of an old Roman road leading to the Romano-British settlement of *Pennocrvcivm* on Watling Street, now the A5.

After 25 metres, turn left through a gap in the hedge and, keeping the hedge on the right, walk up the field to Lapley. Turn left and walk along the road to the churchyard gate. Go through the churchyard with the church on the left, to a stile in a fence on the left behind the church. Go over the stile and walk with the hedge on the left. Past the end of a brick building continue slightly to the right, to regain the hedgerow on the left from where can be seen a bridle gate in the field corner. Go through the bridle gate and continue to walk with the hedge on the left. In the far corner of the field, cross into the next field and continue with the hedge on the left. Just past a pond at the end of a wood on the left, there is a small brick building and just beyond that there is a gap in the hedge on the left. Go through the gap and walk close

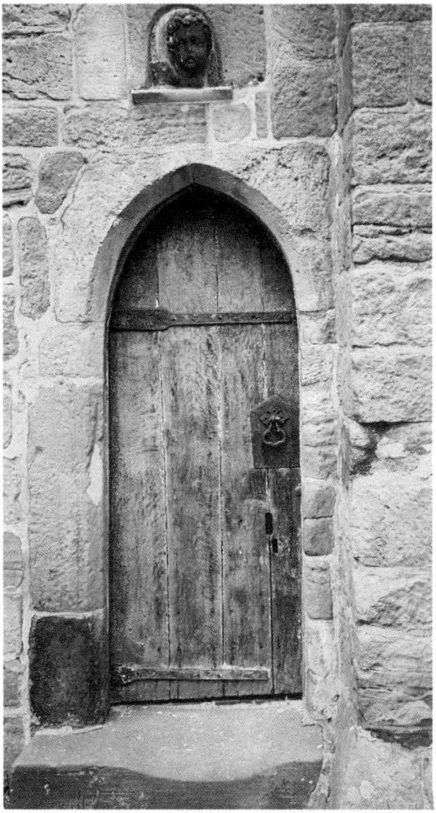

The east door of Lapley church

to the hedge on the right to a bridle gate in the hedge. Go through the gate and a second one immediately behind it. Walk diagonally left to a stile and a gate in the hedge on the left. Do not cross the hedge, but turn right and keep the hedge on the left. Cross a stile in the field corner and continue to the next corner where there are farm buildings on the left behind the hedge.

4. Turn right and follow the hedge on the left. One hundred metres beyond the point where the hedge bends to the left, there is a stile and a gate in the hedge on the left. Go over the stile and walk diagonally right across the corner of the field to a short track through the trees to the next field. Go through the bridle gate ahead and continue with the hedge on the left to a field corner where there is a bridle gate. Go through the bridle gate and enter Bickford Meadows Nature Reserve.

The nature reserve is owned by Staffordshire Wildlife Trust. Bickford Meadows is an example of wet grassland which appears not to have been ploughed or fertilised. Less than 150 examples now remain in Staffordshire due to the intensification of agriculture since the fifties. Those that do remain are mostly on the poorer land of the Peak District.

Follow the path through the meadow and pass into the next field where the path soon follows a raised walkway constructed from old railway sleepers. Where the walkway divides at a T-junction, go left and cross a wooden footbridge. Turn left after the bridge and follow the hedge on the right margin of the field to a gap in the hedge at the top of a slight hill. Go through the gap and continue in the same direction downhill through the middle of the field to the left corner of a wood. Follow the track at the left of the wood and continue to the road at Mitton.

5. Leaving the Staffordshire Way, cross the road and take the road ahead signed Bradley, then after 200 metres, turn left, signed Shredicote. Continue along this farm road, passing Shredicote farm, until after about a mile Shredicote Hall Farm is on the right. This has a large silo in the farm yard.

6. Go through the gate opposite the farm and cross the field diagonally to a stile in the far right corner. Turn left along a green road to two gates. Go through the left gate and continue with the hedge on the right. Cross two stiles to a field. Cross the field, keeping in the same direction, to a bridle gate and a bridge. Cross the bridge and continue with the hedge on the left, crossing two fields to a road. Opposite is a gate into a cottage drive. Inside the gate, turn sharp right, through another gate. Cross a small field diagonally to a stile in the left hedge. Go over the stile and cross the field diagonally to the right, making for a gap in the hedge at the far field corner near a clump of trees. Turn left along the green lane and follow it to the road.

7. Cross the road and follow the track for half a mile (.75 kilometre) to a finger post. Cross the field diagonally right to a gate in the wood. Do not cross the canal bridge but join the tow path.

This is the Shropshire Union canal which connects the Black Country, via Birmingham Canal Navigation and the Staffordshire & Worcestershire canal, with the Mersey at Ellesmere Port.

Turn left and follow the tow path for 2 miles (3 kilometres) to Wheaton Aston. Leave the tow path at the first bridge in Wheaton Aston, bridge number 20. Cross the bridge and follow the track to the road. Continuing in the same direction, walk along the road to a T-junction. Turn left at the T-junction and follow Marston Road to the village hall. Cross the road and the car park is on the left.

Walk 13: Chillington

Dick Ward, Wolverhampton Group

Starting point: Grid reference SJ 880073, Staffordshire County Council car park near Giffard's Cross. To reach the car park from Brewood, turn right after Giffard's Cross.

Distance: 5 miles (8 kilometres) or 4 miles (6.5 kilometres)

Useful maps: Ordnance Survey Pathfinder 891 Wolverhampton(north), or Ordnance Survey Landranger 127 Stafford, Telford and surrounding area

Terrain: Mostly flat, some canal towpath walking.

---

1. From the car park turn left along the lane away from the main road. After about 600 metres join the Staffordshire Way by turning left through a kissing gate into a field. The path runs in a southerly direction along the field boundary and is clearly way-marked. At the end of the field, climb the stile and cross the green lane to a bridge and another stile into the next field. Continue along this field boundary to a finger post in the field corner. Here turn half left and pass a small pond on the left. Follow the path, still way-marked as the Staffordshire Way, to the Codsall to Brewood road. Turn right along the road to the crest of the hill where a road comes in on the right.

2. At this point leave the Staffordshire Way and turn left. This is a private drive along which passes a public bridleway. Go down the bridle path towards Long Birch Farm. This is an avenue of trees which leads down to the farm and passes between the farm on the left and a pond on the right. Follow the concrete roadway for nearly half a mile (700 metres) to the canal.

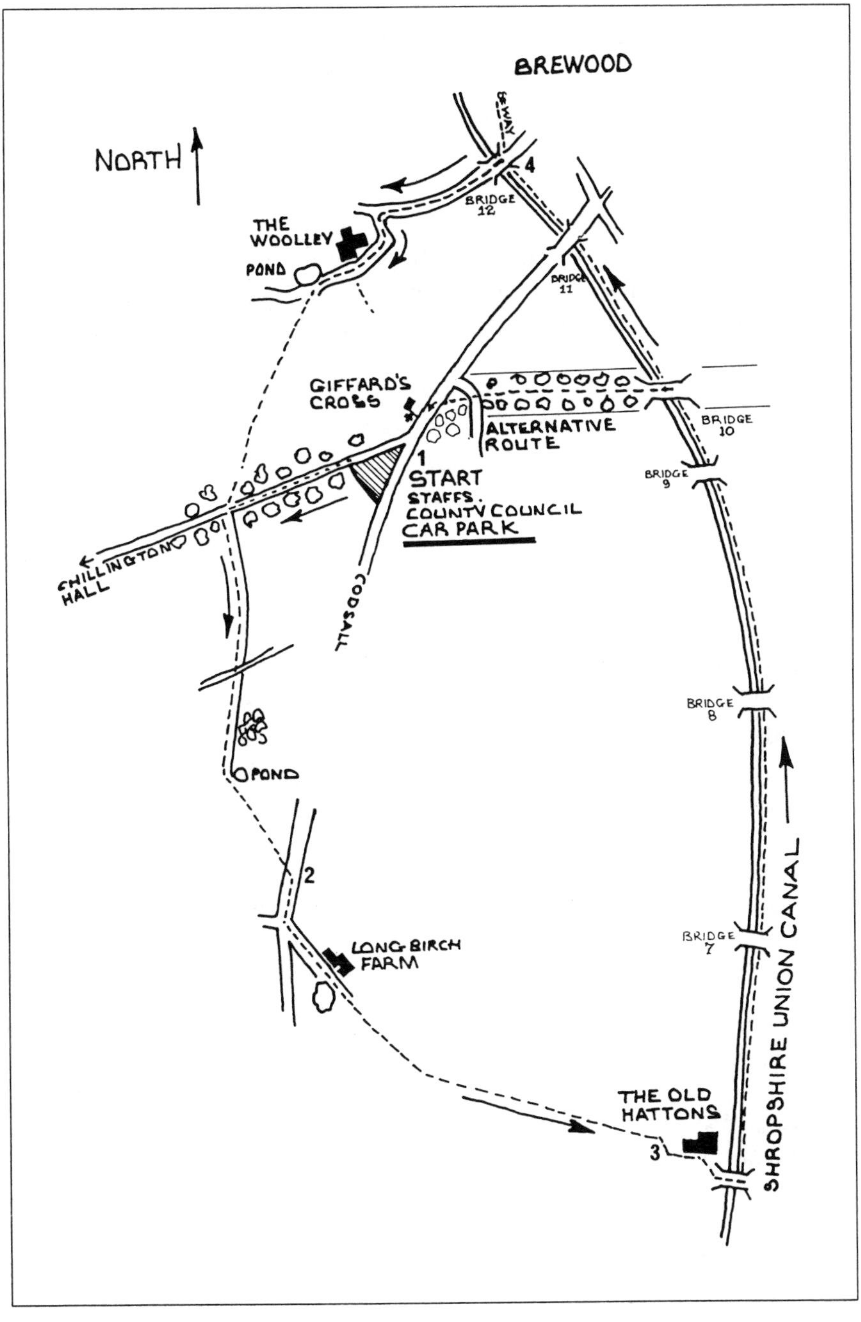
BREWOOD
NORTH
4
BRIDGE 12
THE WOOLLEY
POND
BRIDGE 11
GIFFARD'S CROSS
ALTERNATIVE ROUTE
BRIDGE 10
BRIDGE 9
1
START
STAFFS. COUNTY COUNCIL CAR PARK
CHILLINGTON HALL
CODSALL
BRIDGE 8
POND
2
LONG BIRCH FARM
BRIDGE 7
SHROPSHIRE UNION CANAL
THE OLD HATTONS
3

From this roadway in clear weather there are good views across the M54 to Wolverhampton. It should be possible to pick out landmarks such as St Peter's church and the Mander Centre. Further round to the north east the Post Office tower at Pye Green on Cannock Chase can be seen.

3. At the bottom of the track, walk through Old Hatton Farm and cross the canal by a recently restored bridge. Immediately over the bridge turn left and after 50 metres, join the canal towpath.

This is the Shropshire Union canal which connects the Black Country, via Birmingham Canal Navigation and the Staffordshire & Worcestershire canal, with the Mersey at Ellesmere Port.

Follow the towpath for about a mile, passing bridges 7, 8, and 9, to arrive at bridge 10 in Chillington cutting.

Note the iron bridge guards which protect the soft sandstone of these bridges from erosion by tow-ropes. Bridge 10 is much more ornate with fancy pilasters on the balustrade. This bridge carries the avenue that leads to Chillington Hall and no doubt the Giffards of Chillington wanted to show their wealth.

At bridge number 10 the walk can be shortened by about a mile. Climb the steps leading to this bridge and cross the bridge. Follow the avenue to a small car park, cross the lane and continue along the avenue to come out on the Brewood – Codsall road. Turn left along the road for a short distance and then cross at the T-junction and the car park.

4. Continue through the cutting until bridge number 12. Leave the canal here and go onto the bridge.

From here there is a lovely view of the village of Brewood, dominated by the steeple of the church of St Mary and St Chad.

At this point rejoin the Staffordshire Way which has been following the towpath from the north for some distance. Cross this bridge and follow the lane for about half a mile ($^3/_4$ kilometre). The Staffordshire Way leaves this lane at a stile beyond the farm, opposite a pond. Climb the stile and follow the path alongside the hedge. At the end of the field climb two closely spaced stiles, crossing the end of a belt of trees and come out on to the Avenue.

Away to the right can be seen Chillington Hall, the home of the Giffard family who arrived with William the Conqueror.

Go across the Avenue and soon come to a lane. Turn left along this to return to the car park.

Before leaving, walk up to the main road and turn left along it to the Avenue. A cross in the garden of the gate-house marks the spot where one of the Giffard family killed an escaped panther which was threatening a young lady. This deed is not only commemorated by this cross but is also symbolised on the crest of the Giffard family.

Walk 14: Perton

John Youens, Wolverhampton Group and Geoff Loadwick

Starting point: Grid Reference SO 860003, Perton Lakeside Shopping Centre. Take the A41 road out of Wolverhampton and turn left along Wrottesley Park Road then follow the signs to Perton Centre.

Distance: 7 miles (11.5 kilometres)

Useful maps: Ordnance Survey Pathfinder 891 Wolverhampton (north), and Pathfinder 912 Wolverhampton (south), or Ordnance Survey Landranger 127 Stafford, Telford & surrounding Area and Landranger 139 Birmingham

Terrain: Flat with wide open spaces and little shelter from the wind

---

1. Leave the car park at the side of Sainsbury's petrol station and turn right to walk along Coleridge Drive. At the end of Coleridge Drive, by the mini-roundabout, turn right and take the first road on the left, Mercia Drive. Just after passing Penda Grove, turn right to follow a pedestrian way passing between a bungalow and the neighbouring house. The tarmac path ends at Dippon's Lane, an old tree-lined lane. Cross over Dippon's Lane into a tree lined track and after 125 metres turn left onto a footpath.

Follow the footpath to a stile at the side of a narrow road. Cross the stile and go over the road to cross the ditch via a little footbridge. Continue along the path that leads between a barbed wire fence on the right and vegetation on the left to a stile. Cross the stile and enter a field. Follow the hedge on the left until it ends and then walk across the narrow neck of field to a stile under a large oak in the hedge opposite. Climb over the stile and walk diagonally right to a stile in the corner of the field. The stile gives access to a lane. Turn right to follow the lane to the end of the road at a T-junction.

2. Turn left and walk past the drive of a house called The Orchard. Keeping the buildings on the left, follow the road as it bends to the left and enter the drive to The Grange. Where the drive turns left, continue straight on along a bridleway.

   This bridleway was part of the old coach road to Shrewsbury and thence to Holyhead from London. It was by-passed by the turnpike road, now the A41 Holyhead Road that lies a little to the north, and re-joins the former route as the A464 at its junction with County Road near the Summer House public house.

   Go through a bridle gate or over the stile at the side of the gate and continue along the broad green track bordered with large oaks on both sides. The bridleway enters the garden of a derelict house and leaves almost immediately through tall iron gates. Beyond the house, continue along the bridleway, which shows signs of once having been surfaced with tarmac. The bridleway leads through the trees to a road.

3. Cross the road and continue along the bridleway. Where the old tarmac ends, continue in the same direction along the right hand edge of an extremely large field. At the far corner of the field, turn left and walk along a track with a conifer plantation on the right. Go past the end of the conifer plantation and continue along the track to a T-junction at the corner of a small group of horse-chestnut trees. Turn right and almost immediately pass a pond on the left hand side. In less than 300 metres there is a second pond.
   Just past this pond, the Staffordshire Way crosses the track. Turn right to follow the Staffordshire Way briefly across the field past the foot of a solitary oak to a track in front of the hedgerow beyond. Turn left, leaving the Staffordshire Way. The track passes to the right of a small lake where it swings right and immediately left to continue with a hedge on the left. At the T-junction turn right.

4. Ignore the turn off to the left and follow a tree-lined drive

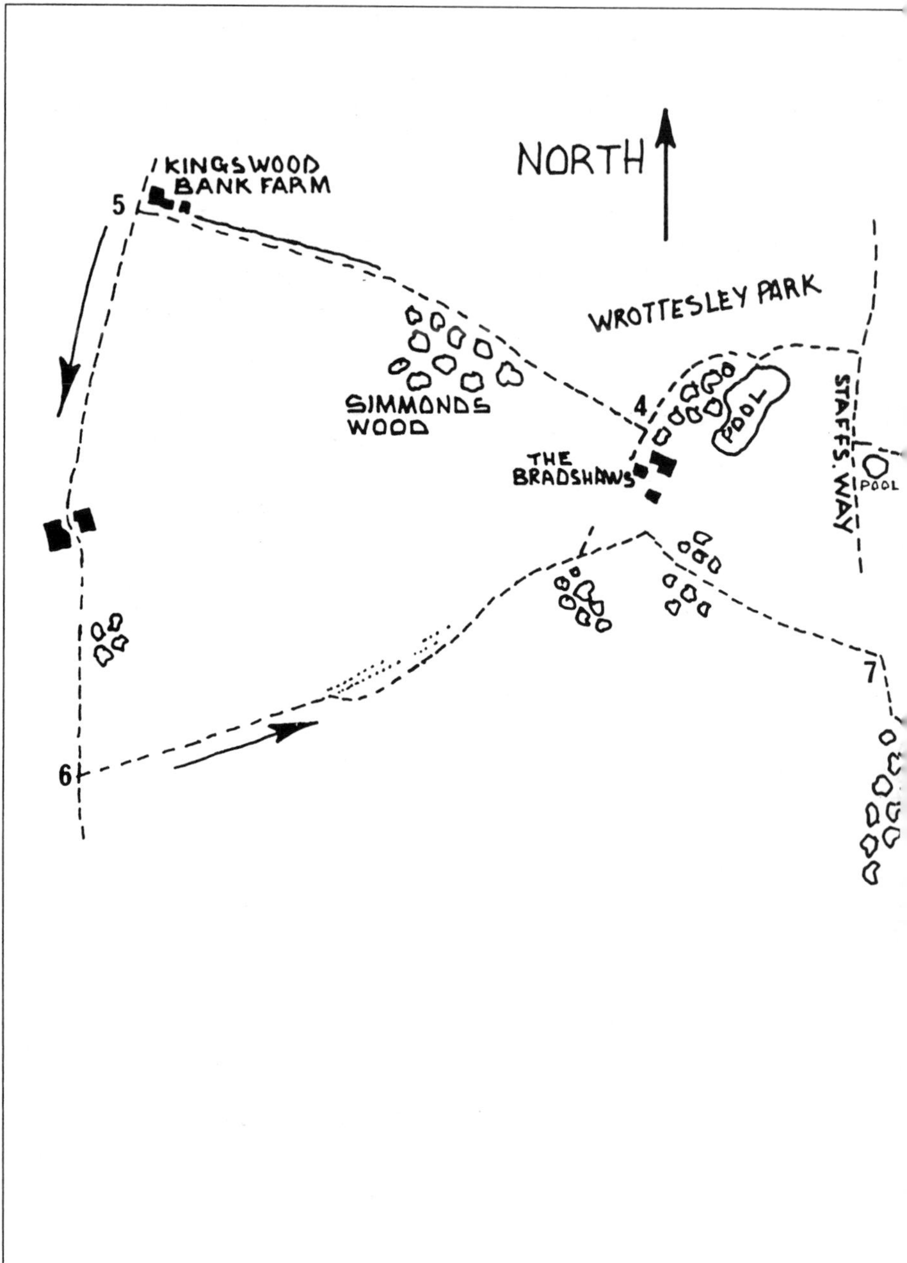
KINGSWOOD BANK FARM
NORTH
5
WROTTESLEY PARK
SIMMONDS WOOD
4
POOL
THE BRADSHAWS
STAFFS. WAY
POOL
7
6

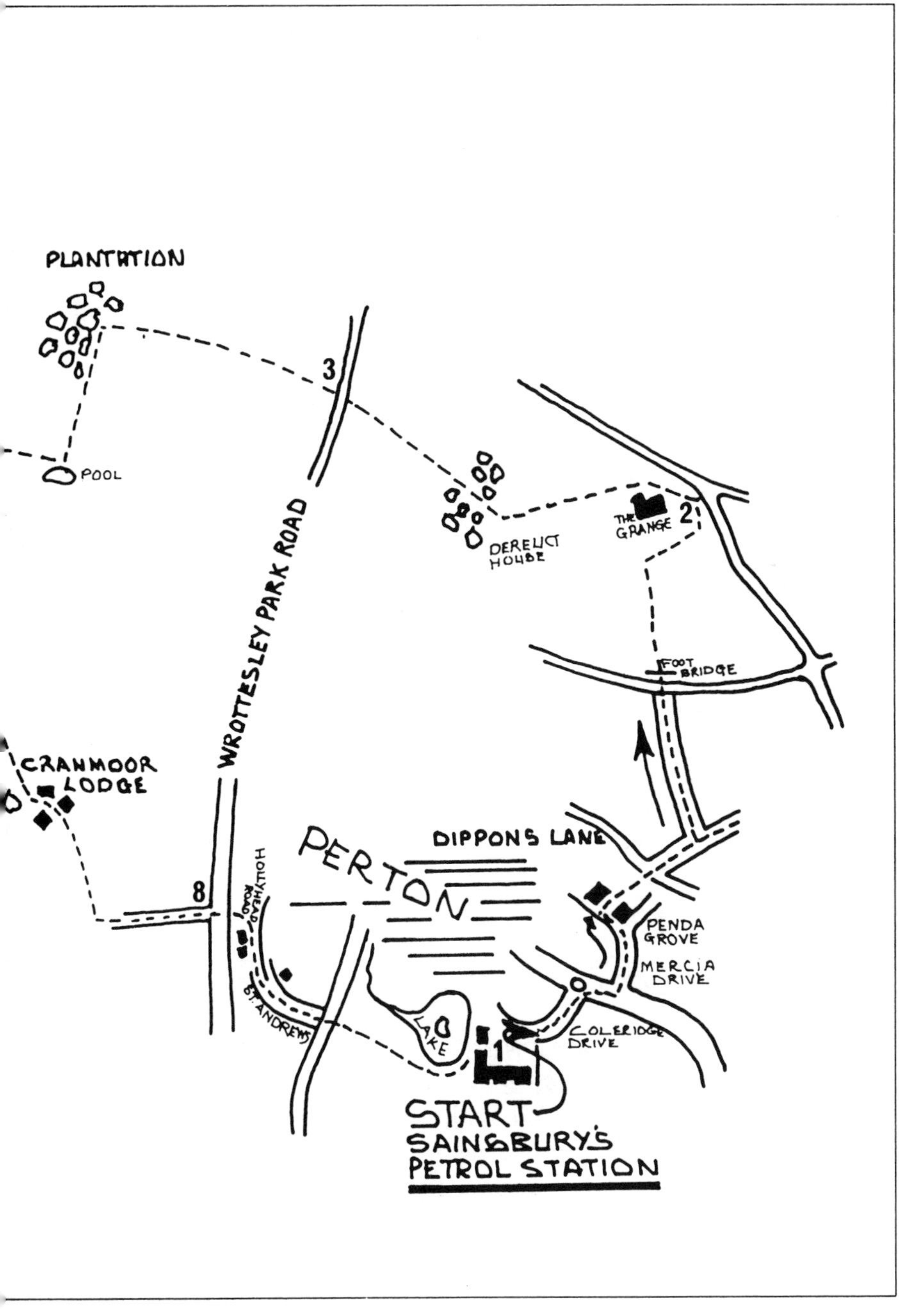
PLANTATION
POOL
3
WROTTESLEY PARK ROAD
DERELICT HOUSE
THE GRANGE
2
FOOT BRIDGE
CRANMOOR LODGE
8
PERTON
DIPPONS LANE
HOLLYHEAD ROAD
ST. ANDREWS
LAKE
1
PENDA GROVE
MERCIA DRIVE
COLERIDGE DRIVE
START
SAINSBURY'S
PETROL STATION

which is a bridleway. Ignore the first turn-off to the right and go straight ahead at the next junction. Ignore the turn to the left at the corner of a small wood but continue for a further fifty metres to a bridle gate in the field corner. Go through the gate and follow the grass track along an avenue of trees. At the end of the avenue of trees there is a gate across the end of a track. Go through the gate and walk along the track. Pass a house on the right and continue along the drive which leads directly into a tarmac lane. Follow the lane to a T-junction and turn left.

There are extensive views to the right. The Wrekin can easily be distinguished, although it appears much flatter from this side, and on a clear day, to the left of the Wrekin can be seen a panorama of Shropshire Hills including Brown Clee and Titterstone Clee. The cooling towers of Buildwas power station can also be seen. The road that runs parallel to this lane, just a field away on the right is "County Lane"; an ancient lane that wriggles along the boundary between Shropshire and Staffordshire.

5. Follow the lane to pass between the buildings of Wrottesley Lodge Farm and continue beyond the edge of the tarmac. The track passes a small oak wood and just before reaching another wood ahead, there is a track on the left. Turn onto this track.

In good weather you may enjoy a view which includes Wolverhampton and Sedgley Beacon to the south-east.

6. The track runs along the edge of a field and continues with a coppice on the left to the estate yard at The Bradshaws. At the edge of the estate yard turn right at a vehicle inspection ramp to walk past the side of a low building. Where the track divides three ways, take the middle track across the field. The route joins the Staffordshire Way at the hedgerow.

7. Go through the hedge and turn right to follow the Stafford-

Pool near Wrottesley Hall

shire Way along the edge of the field and then along a path between hedges. When the red brick building of Cranmoor Lodge appears 100 metres ahead, do not turn right to follow the Staffordshire Way, but continue along the grassy lane with the hedge on the left. At Cranmoor Lodge, turn left and walk between brick walls. When the wall on the left ends, turn right between the buildings and follow the drive away from the lodge. Continue along the drive to the road.

8. Cross the busy road carefully and turn left. Follow the verge for 25 metres to the end of a wooden fence and turn right along a path that goes behind houses to emerge at the end of a cul-de-sac. Walk to the end of the road, Hoylake Road, and turn right. Follow the road, St Andrew's Road, to the end. Cross the road and follow the infant river Penk to an artificial lake. Walk anti-clockwise round the lake to reach the starting point.

Walk 15: Enville and the Sheepwalks

John Gilmer, Stourbridge Group

Starting point: Grid Reference SO 825868, public car park on the corner of Blundies Lane and the A458, Bridgnorth Road, in Enville.

Distance: 5 miles (8 kilometres)

Useful maps: Ordnance Survey Pathfinder 933 Stourbridge & Kinver, or Ordnance Survey Landranger 138 Kidderminster and Wyre Forest.

Terrain: Mostly flat but with one moderate climb to the top of the Sheepwalks.

---

1. From the car park return to the main road and turn right up the hill to go past the former Enville primary school on the right and Enville church on the left.

   Enville primary school was built in 1861 with funds provided by the Countess of Stamford and Warrington who lived at Enville Hall. St Mary's church, restored between 1872 and 1875 by Sir Gilbert Scott, has a fine Somerset-Grain tower and contains some high quality decorative woodwork.

   With great care, continue along the right side of the road. The grass verge widens after the first bend. Join the Staffordshire Way at the driveway of a house called Enville Court, where there is a footpath sign. Turn right into the drive and follow the boundary on the left across the grass to a white hand-gate in the far corner. Go through the gate and follow the track over two stiles and a foot bridge and continue along the right edge of a field to a stile giving access to the road.

2. Cross the road and go over the stile at the side of a gate.

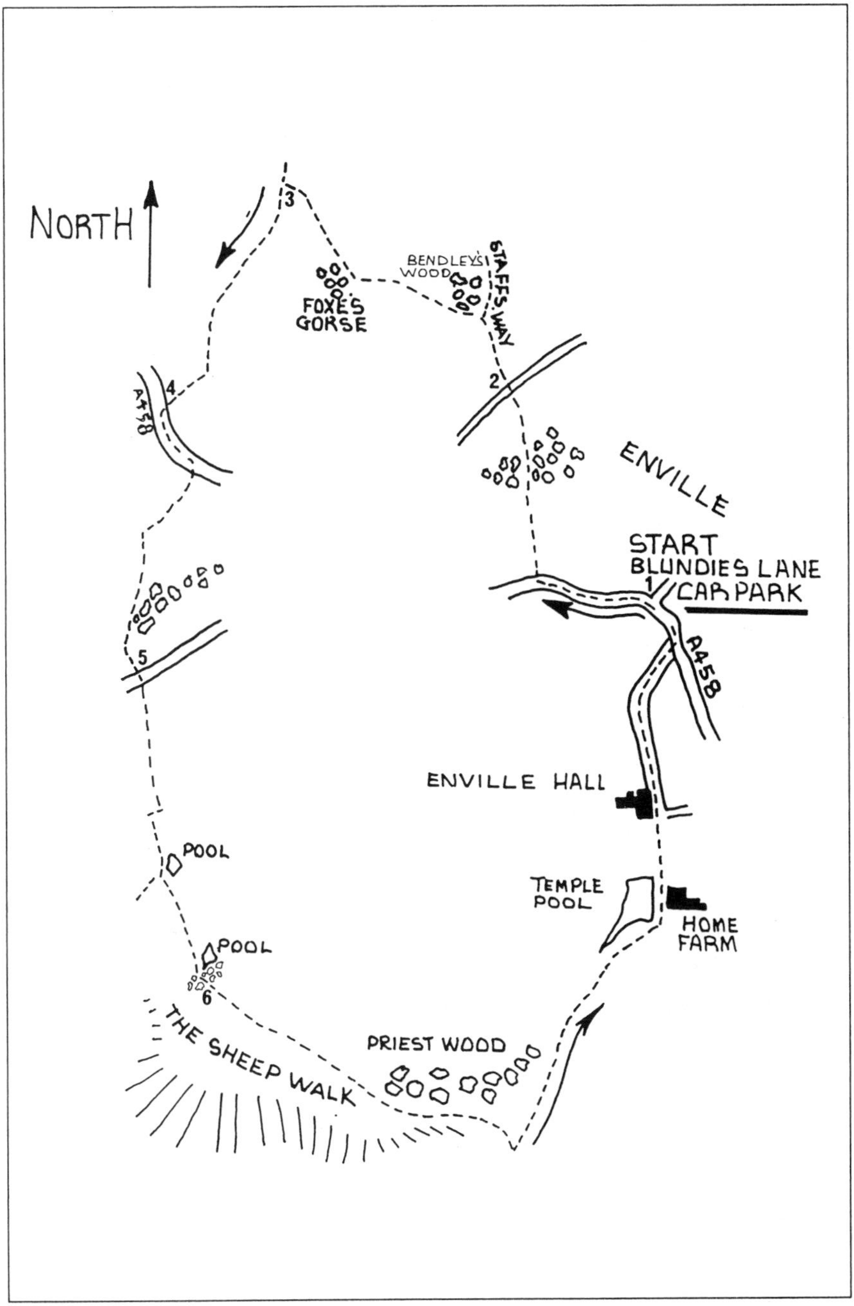
NORTH
3
BENDLEY'S WOOD
STAFFS WAY
FOXES GORSE
4
A458
2
ENVILLE
START
BLUNDIES LANE
1
CAR PARK
A458
5
ENVILLE HALL
POOL
TEMPLE POOL
HOME FARM
POOL
6
THE SHEEP WALK
PRIEST WOOD

Continue along the left edge of the field for 250 metres to two stiles in the double hedgeline on the left. Cross both stiles, leaving the Staffordshire Way, and walk diagonally to the right to a stile next to a gate on the left of a wood. Cross the stile and continue walking in the same direction diagonally across the field to a stile in the far corner. Continue across the corner of the next field to two gates at the corner of a wood. Go through the gate on the right and follow a broad track along the right side of the wood. After a while, the track bends to the left and dips slightly downhill to a T-junction of tracks.

3. Turn left and go through a gateway. Follow the broad track past a small pool on the left. Just after the pool, the track turns right and leads through an avenue of poplars. Just before reaching a field corner that juts out from the left, there is a stile on the left under an oak. Cross the stile and with the hedge on the right walk to the next field corner where there is another stile. Cross this stile and continue with the hedge on the right. Near where the hedge bends to the left, there is a stile in the hedgeline. Cross the stile and walk for 25 metres with the hedge on the left and then turn right and walk across the field to a single power line pole that has a stile at its base. Go over the stile and cross the paddock to reach the A458 road.

4. Cross the road carefully and turn left. After approximately 200 metres, there is a footpath sign on the right and three gateways giving access to adjacent fields. Go through the middle gateway and follow the hedge at the left into the far corner of the field where there is a double stile. Go over both stiles and walk directly to the field corner jutting out on the right and continue to the next corner, jutting out on the left. From here walk to the next corner jutting out on the left and turn left to follow the hedge to a gate giving access to the road.

5. Cross the road and go down the track opposite. At the end of the track, continue across a narrow field to a stile. Go over the stile and bear right through a tunnel of trees to emerge in a

Temple Pool

field on the left. Walk with the hedgeline on the left and follow it round the corner of the field to a gap in the hedge. Go through the gap and cross the track on the other side of the hedge. Walk down the slope and up the other side to meet the left hand hedge at the top of the slope. Follow the hedge round the bottom corner of the field as it passes to the right of a pool. Just past the pool there is a stile partially hidden in the trees on the left giving access to an open area known as the Sheepwalks.

6. Cross the stile and follow the marker posts uphill to the top of the Sheepwalks.

This is a steep climb but on a clear day the reward is well worth the effort. Rest a while and admire the views of the Malvern Hills to the south and the Wrekin to the west.

From the top of the hill, continue following the marker posts to a stile next to a gate. Go over the stile and follow the boundary on the right to a stile in the fence on the right. Do not go over the stile but turn left, away from the stile and walk across the slope of the hill to the left corner of a wood ahead. Go over the stile on the right just beyond the corner of the wood and turn left to follow a track downhill to a lake. Walk with the lake on the left, crossing a small paddock and passing between a building and the lake. Continue to the corner of the field just to the right of Enville Hall where there is a stile next to the wall giving access to a track. Here the route re-joins the Staffordshire way. Follow the track past the hall to emerge at the Cat Inn in Enville village. Cross the road carefully and turn left to return to the car park.

At the end of the 19th century, the Gardens of Enville Hall were extensive. They occupied the attentions of a head gardener and thirty-five men whose total wage bill amounted to £100 per week.

Walk 16: Kinver Edge

Geoff Loadwick, Stoke/Newcastle Group

Starting point: Grid Reference SK 846833, Acre car park opposite the Pharmacy in High Street, Kinver. This car park might be closed on Sundays but there are other car parks in the vicinity.

Distance: 6 miles (9.5 kilometres)

Useful maps: Ordnance Survey Pathfinder 933 Stourbridge & Kinver, or Ordnance Survey Landranger 138 Kidderminster and Wyre Forest and Landranger 139 Birmingham

Terrain: There are some steep gradients at the beginning of the walk approaching Kinver Edge and at the end of the walk descending to the car park, otherwise the ground is gently undulating. Some tracks, particularly the bridleways, will be muddy after wet weather.

---

1. Leave the car park and turn left into High Street. Turn left in front of the public library to follow the tarmac road, a public footpath, up the hill. Where the road divides three ways, follow the stony track on the right. This is a private drive with a pedestrian right of way. At the entrance to the Old Vicarage, turn left and go through a metal gate to follow a narrow track to the road. Turn right and follow the pavement past a school. Where the footpath runs out, cross the road to the footpath on the other side and follow it up the hill. Cross the end of Forrest Drive to reach a T-junction and turn left along Stone Lane. Continue along Compton Road.

On the left there is a plaque commemorating the "giant's well" from which the water ran into a stone trough and provided the parishioners of Kinver with a plentiful water supply for many centuries. The well had to be abandoned when the housing estate was built in 1956.

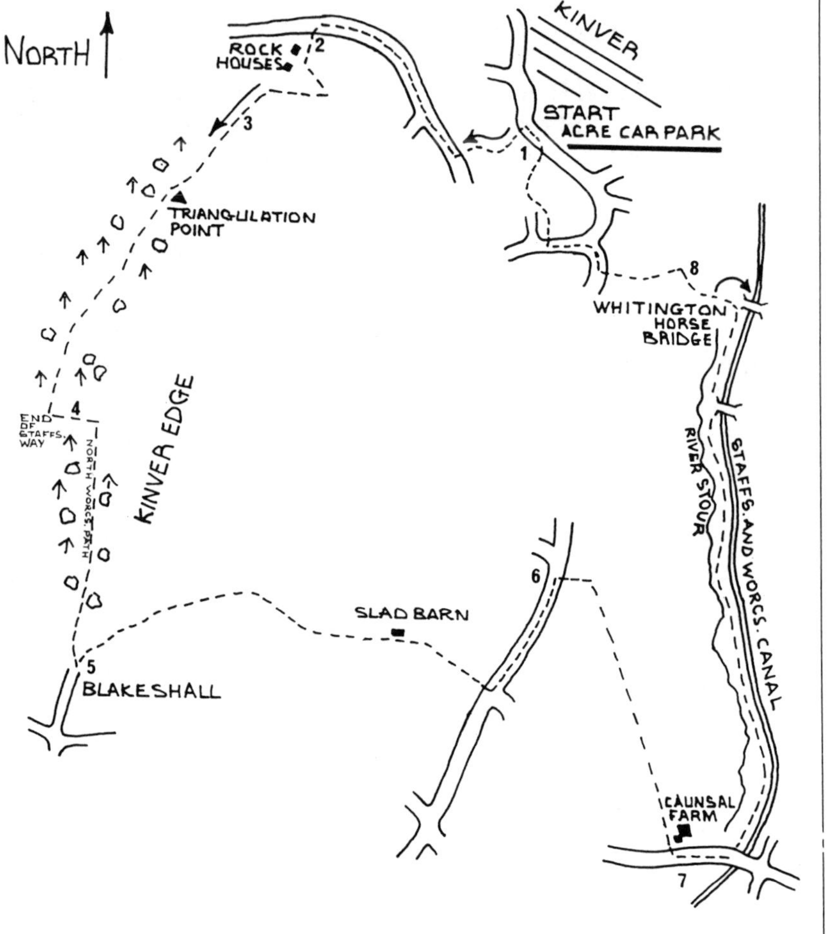
NORTH
KINVER
ROCK HOUSES
2
START
ACRE CAR PARK
1
3
TRIANGULATION POINT
8
WHITINGTON HORSE BRIDGE
KINVER EDGE
4
END OF STAFFS. WAY
NORTH WORCS. PATH
RIVER STOUR
STAFFS. AND WORCS. CANAL
6
SLAD BARN
5
BLAKESHALL
CAUNSAL FARM
7

2. Shortly after passing the road called "Edge Hill" and before the speed derestriction sign is reached, turn left up the stony track marked by a footpath sign. The track leads to the old rock houses now in the care of the National Trust.

   These rock houses at Holy Austin Rock were occupied by twelve families in the 1850's and became a tourist attraction in the early 1900's. Several occupants provided teas and the last café closed as recently as 1967. The name Holy Austin may refer to a hermitage first recorded in the 16th century.

   From the entrance to the rock houses several paths lead up to the ridge. Take any of the paths on the left and follow it up through the wood to enter a grassy clearing. In the clearing, swing round to the right and follow the ridge up through the trees to another, larger clearing where there is a toposcope showing the directions and distances of places of interest. The Staffordshire Way climbs the western slopes of Kinver Edge and meets the ridge at this point.

   This clearing formed part of an 11 acre Iron Age fort that was built about 2500 years ago. It was defended on two sides by a substantial bank and ditch and on the other two sides by the edge of the escarpment. Look out for the remains of an earth bank as you continue the walk. Just below this bank there is another construction of military significance; the square brick building was a Home Guard post during the Second World War.

3. Continue along the ridge following the Staffordshire Way, taking care not to be diverted along any side paths. Past the triangulation pillar the ground begins to drop away steeply on the right and there are good views towards the Clent Hills on the left. Go through the horse barrier at the edge of the National Trust property and continue down to another horse barrier at the county boundary. Here there is a large signpost indicating the end of the Staffordshire Way and its junction with two other long distance paths.

The two other paths are the North Worcestershire Path which goes off to the left, and the Worcestershire Way which continues ahead along the ridge. The North Worcestershire Path extends 28 miles to Forhill and the Worcestershire Way which is 32 miles long, goes to Malvern.

4. At the County boundary, turn left to follow the North Worcestershire Path. At the first crossing of paths, turn right to go through a horse barrier and continue down a broad forest path. Soon the North Worcestershire path turns to the left but ignore this turning and go on down the broad path to a point where it appears to divide into four main paths. There is a cross path and two others that continue ahead. Take the path on the left that continues ahead and follow it across a bridleway, where the path is guarded by horse barriers, and down to another barrier. Go past the barrier to join a track that comes in from the left and continue in the same direction to the road at Blakeshall. Just before the road is reached, the track splits into two. Ignore the branch on the left.

5. At the road, turn left and almost immediately there is a bridleway on the right. Ignore this bridleway and continue along the road to the next bend where there is another bridleway on the right. Follow this bridleway. After a few metres, the track broadens momentarily where it is crossed by a footpath. Ignore this footpath and continue along the bridleway down the hill to the road. Turn left and follow the surfaced footpath at the side of the road. Just before Gipsy Lane is reached, there is a marker post in the hedge on the left indicating the North Worcestershire Path. There is a corresponding signpost on the right.

6. Cross the road to the stile beside a metal gate and go over the stile into the field. The path follows the left edge of the field to a two-legged electricity pole and then turns right to cross the field. The path continues along the left boundary of two more fields and then crosses a series of stiles at the side of Caunsall Farm before emerging at a road by the farm entrance.

7. Turn left and cross the River Stour. Shortly afterwards turn left just before the canal bridge and follow the towpath.

James Brindley, the father of canals in Britain, had an ambition to join the four great rivers, Mersey, Trent, Severn and Thames by inland waterways. The Staffordshire & Worcestershire Canal, whose construction was authorised in 1766, was part of this scheme. It joins the Trent & Mersey Canal to the Severn at Stourport but it was not until 1790, seventeen years after Brindley's death that the scheme was completed with a link to the Thames at Oxford.

Cross the road at Whittington Bridge, Number 27, and continue along the towpath at the other side. Leave the towpath at the next bridge, Whitting Horse Bridge, by turning left along the track that passes in front of the cottage. The track changes to a tarmac road as it passes the Anchor hotel.

8. Go through the kissing gate opposite the second house on the right and cross the field slightly to the right to reach a fence corner. Follow the hedge round the corner keeping it on the right. In the next corner there is wooden gate on the right. Go through the gate and follow the narrow path to the road. Turn right and then immediately left towards St Peter's Church.

St Peter's church dates from the 14th century and is well worth a visit. It has an unusually shaped 14th century font and some splendid early 16 century brasses of Sir Edward grey and his family.

Take the first turning on the right to walk over a cattle grid into the church yard. Follow the drive up to the corner of the church where just to the right there is a public footpath sign. Go through the gap in the wall and descend the steep path. Go straight over the cross path and down the brick steps at the side of a house to reach Acre car park once again.

Useful Information

Travel information

Staffordshire County Council can supply information about bus and train services in the area. Enquiries should be addressed to: Staffordshire County Council, Highways House, Riverway, Stafford. ST16 3TJ. Telephone (01785) 223344

Touring Centres

It is not possible to reach all the walks conveniently by using public transport. For those travelling by private car, all the walks are within an hour's drive of Stafford but visitors to the area, wishing to gain a more authentic impression of the varied nature of the county, would be better advised to use several different centres. The following towns and villages would make convenient places to stay, for the walks indicated:

Leek	walks 1,2,3
Oakamoor or Alton	walks 4,5,6;
Abbots Bromley	walks 7,8,9
Brewood	walks 12,13,14
Kinver	walks 15 and 16

Accommodation

A Staffordshire Way accommodation guide is obtainable free of charge from Christine Cheeseman, Department of Cultural and Recreational Services, Staffordshire County Council, Shire Hall, Market Street, Stafford. ST16 2LQ. Telephone (01785) 277247.

'Where to stay along the Staffordshire Way' is published by the Staffordshire Area of the Ramblers' Association. Copies can be obtained from the Ramblers' Association Central Office.

Ramblers' Association

Membership enquiries, footpath problem reports, and requests for accommodation leaflets should be addressed to:

Ramblers' Association Central Office, 1/5 Wandsworth Road, London. SW8 2XX. Telephone 0170 582 6878

Path problems

If when using this book, you find any obstructions or problems of access on rights of way in Staffordshire, or on concessionary paths on the Staffordshire Way, it would be helpful to report the details to Staffordshire County Council with copies to the Ramblers' Association. Photocopies of the form overleaf can be used to make reports to Staffordshire County Council. Any problems encountered on that part of the Kinver Edge walk which lies in Worcestershire, can be reported to Len Chambers, Rights of Way Officer, Public Rights of Way Section, Hereford & Worcestershire County Council, County Hall, Spetchley Road, Worcester WR5 2NP. Telephone: 01905 766877

Guide Books to the Staffordshire Way

"The Staffordshire Way". £5.00 plus 40p post and packing per book, from Department of Cultural and Recreational Services, Staffordshire County Council, Shire Hall, Market Street, Stafford. ST16 2LQ. Telephone: (01785) 277247. Make cheques payable to Staffordshire County Council.

"The Staffordshire Way" by Les Lumsdon and Chris Rushton, from Sigma Leisure and all good booksellers price £6.95. ISBN: 1 85058 315 3.

FOOTPATH/BRIDLEWAY PROBLEM REPORT

Please send completed forms to:

The County Countryside Officer,
Staffordshire County Council,
Shire Hall,
Market Street,
Stafford. ST16 2LQ

1. Your name and address.

NAME: ____________________

____

ADDRESS: ____________________

____

____

2. Where was the problem?

DISTRICT: ____________________

PARISH: ____________________

PATH FROM (PLACE): ____________________

(GRID REFERENCE): ____________________

TO (PLACE): ____________________

(GRID REFERENCE): ____________________

PATH NUMBER (IF KNOWN): ____________________

3. When did you meet the problem?

DATE PROBLEM WAS ENCOUNTERED: ____________________

4. If anyone spoke to you, please give details including their name and address if possible

Report form side 1

FOOTPATH/BRIDLEWAY PROBLEM REPORT

5. What was the problem? Be precise and quote a grid reference for any specific point. Draw a sketch map if you think it will help.

Report form side 2

ALSO OF INTEREST . . .

TEASHOP WALKS IN THE PEAK DISTRICT

This guidebook contains twenty-six varied and attractive walks suitable for all the family. June and Norman Buckley describe them with accurate instructions, clear sketch maps and delightful photographs. To add to the pleasure, each walk includes one or more teashops; ranging from a homely farmhouse kitchen to a converted cotton mill. The walks are spaced throughout the Peak District. There are strolls in the peaceful valleys of Dovedale, Lathkill Dale and Miller's Dale, high-level walks up Shutlingsloe, the 'Matterhorn of Cheshire', and along the Roaches, and visits to such typical Peakland towns and villages as Bakewell and Tissington. *£6.95*

BEST STAFFORDSHIRE WALKS

Les Lumsdon is a Senior Lecturer in tourism at the University of Staffordshire and knows his county like the back of his hand. He has also completely revised and up-dated his book to produce this new edition of a popular collection of country walks. *£6.95*

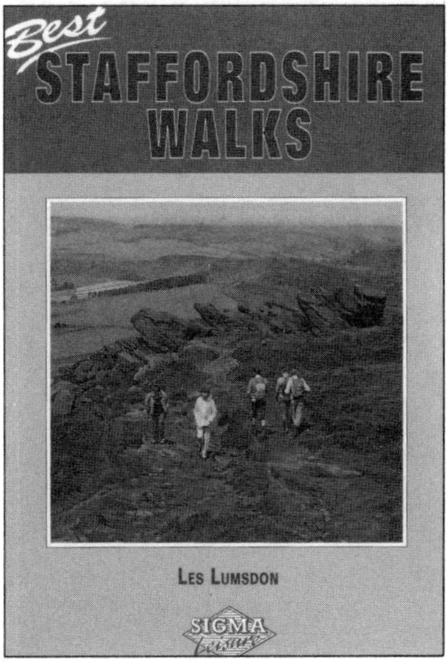

BEST PUB WALKS IN NORTH STAFFORDSHIRE

Les Lumsdon joins forces with local photographer Chris Rushton to produce this super collection of walks that are all based on popular local hostelries. Varied walks, excellent pubs and real ale all combine to make perfect days out. *£6.95*

BEST PUB WALKS IN SOUTH STAFFORDSHIRE

This South Staffs companion , due in 1997, completes our coverage of Staffs pub walks: discover the charm of country walks in the traditional home of real ale. *£6.95*

You can order our books from your local bookshop and we also supply by mail order. Please add £2 p&p (UK).

Sigma Leisure, 1 South Oak Lane, Wilmslow, Cheshire, SK9 6AR.
Tel: 01625-531035; Fax: 01625-536800

Our complete on-line catalogue is on the Internet:

http://www.sigmapress.co.uk